SEARS 16
SEARS LIST OF SUBJECT HEADINGS

About the Author

Mohinder Partap Satija currently on the teaching faculty of the Guru Nanak Dev University is in library profession for the last 27 years. He is the auther of more than a dozen books and about 100 paper published in Indian and foreign library journals. In some of his work he has collaborated with international experts. He has visited Germany, Finland, England, Nepal, the Netherlands, and Belgium in connection with professional work. He is associated with many library journals such as *Information Management Report* (Elsevier, UK), *Library Times International* (USA) the *Lukhnow Librarian* (India), *Asian Libraries* (UK) and *Knowledge Organisation* (USA/Germeny). He is the Indian Coordinator of the *International Society for knowledge Organisation* (ISKO) (the Netherlands). Dr. Satija is a life member of many library and information science associations; and has delivered lectures in many universities. He served as a Visiting Fellow for three months in Maastricht McLuhan Institute, University of Maastricht in the summer of 1999.

SEARS 16
SEARS LIST OF SUBJECT HEADINGS
A Practical Introduction for Indian Students

M. P. SATIJA

CONCEPT PUBLISHING COMPANY, NEW DELHI-110055

ISBN 81-7022-844-1 (HP)

First Published 2000

Published and Printed by
Ashok Kumar Mittal
Concept Publishing Company
A/15-16, Commercial Block, Mohan Garden
New Delhi-110059 (India)

Phones : 5648039, 5649024
Fax : 091-(11) - 5648053.
Email : publishing@conceptpub.com

Dedicated
with profound regards
to
Kim H Veltman
A Scholar of Art, Media and Digital Culture

PREFACE

Library users' requirements are complex; documents are complex. New temporal and conceptual linkages between concepts require new insights and dexterity on the part of information services professionals to collect, analyse, describe, represent and retrieve intellectual contents of knowledge through our systems. We have to know our users and improve the efficiency of our systems to serve them in the dynamically changing environment. Unprecedented growth and diversity of knowledge has thrown up many challenges and opportunities for the library and information services profession.

To facilitate new knowledge through research we need to provide easy and exhaustive access to the already known knowledge. Acute proliferation and complexity of knowledge makes its organisation a demanding task. Inevitably in such a flood of information, knowledge and documents, most of the approaches to the information store will be for unknown items–searches offered by the subject access systems. Therefore, potential usefulness of information storage and retrieval system cannot be exploited fully without properly designed subject catalogues. Subject headings which may be described as heart of the subject catalogues though based on well drawn out principles turn out to be an art, an intuitive craft as Eric Coates is wont to say. At times it is intellectual work of high order in library and information services.

A list of subject headings is a small component in the complex information processing and retrieval system. The *Sears List* is an outstanding name in subject headings lists used all over the world in small and medium size libraries. It has constantly been revised to keep it up to date both in its methods and contents. It has continually incorporated new subjects coming out turbulently. Being handy, simple, inexpensive and always current, the Sears has come as an obvious choice for teaching subject headings work in library schools especially in the Third World countries. Accordingly there is enough literature on the system especially in the form of chapters in books on cataloguing, subject analysis and knowledge organisation. For reasons not clearly known there has been no exclusive book on using the Sears List except, now a long dated:

An Introduction to Sears List of Subject Headings/ by Philip R D Corrigan. London : Clive Bingley, 1967. VII, 94p. (A programmed text in library and information science).

Based on 9th edition (1965) of the Sears it was an excellent and the only textbook on the subject.

The present work is an endeavour to fill a glaring gap in our literature. It provides a companion workbook to Sears-16 to explain its theoretical moorings, history and practical operations. It explains the various hidden potentials of the system to coin subject headings. To be simple, clear and amply illustrative is the object of this small practical introduction. The present book assumes no prior knowledge either of the Sears List or of subject headings work on part of its users. It is an instruction book for the beginners to understand the importance of vocabulary control, the process of subject analysis, the structure and organization of the Sears-16 (1997), and the method to locate, specify, and coin anew unenumerated subject headings and provide cross reference for public catalogue. Subject headings in languages, literatures, biographical and geographical works are given as illustrations to depict the hidden potentials of the system.

The Sears is a long list as well as machine to coin subject headings. Learning to deftly operate the machine makes the SH work stimulating and intellectually challenging. Therefore, the book aims at the working cataloguers to explore the hidden vast capacity to turn out subject headings; and to explain the subtleties and nuances of the system. It might encourage the cataloguers from non-western cultures to explore and adapt Sears to coin headings suited to their culture and literature.

At the same time the Sears systems has many inconsistencies and omissions. Many clarifications are explicitly needed. For example, are the topical subdivisions applicable to the narrower terms or the headings derived according to SA instructions? There is no explicit statement to make a language family name a subject heading. Above all, just like any other subject analysis tool the Sears is inherently biased towards Western (dominantly American), Christian and capitalistic culture. *For example,* heading for Unmarried mothers/fathers, Single Parent family, or Children of divorced parents are there, for which no literature is available in India. But child marriage, which is a current concern in India finds no mention in the list.

This workbook with so many explanations and illustrations aims to help the cataloguers and students to have a joyous times working with the Sears to analyse and represent knowledge and appreciate its flexibility to coin standard subject headings for Indian libraries.

M.P.S

ACKNOWLEDGEMENTS

Part of this work was completed in 1999 during the Visiting Fellowship granted by the Maastricht McLuhan Institute (MMI), University of Maastricht. The wonderful and rich Dahlberg Library of the MMI provided almost everything under one roof to do such a work. Grateful thanks are to the MMI Directors Anneke Eurlings and Kim H Veltman for providing every needed facility in a congenial and inspiring environment. Thanks to all other staff of the MMI especially Nik Baerten, Jo Beerens and Hannie Spronck for their friendly help to make my stay comfortable there.

Joseph Miller, Ingetraut Dahlberg, Krishan Kumar, R.G. Prasher and Paivi Pekkarinen encouraged me to undertake this work. Ranbir Kaur, Director Pioneer Computers, Amritsar gave shape to my almost illegible longhand and was never tired of frequent additions and alterations. It is always a pleasure to see her fast fingers dancing effortlessly on the keyboard. Ashok Mittal, Managing Director, M/s Concept Publishing Company deserves thanks for publishing this work in such a short time.

M.P. SATIJA

CONTENTS

1

HISTORY OF THE SEARS LIST AND SALIENT FEATURES OF THE SEARS-16

A standard and popular subject cataloguing tool for full quarter of a century, Sears list was first designed in 1923 by Minnie Earl Sears (1873-1933) in deference to demands of small libraries for simple and broader subject heading for use in their dictionary catalogues. It was based on a survey of subject heading practices of nine small but well catalogued libraries. Published from the very beginning by H.W. Wilson Company–by then an established and reputed vendor of library products and services–it was meant for small libraries which found Library of Congress Subject Headings too detailed and wide of the mark. It was indicated so in the title of the first through sixth edition (1950): *List of Subject Headings for Small Libraries: Compiled from List Used in Nine Representative Small Libraries.* The first edition culled 3203 preferred headings from catalogues of these libraries. The technical model was and still is the *Library of Congress Subject Headings*, 1909–. It was the policy of Miss Sears to use the LC form of subject headings with some modifications chiefly the simplification of phrases. The policy has been followed unswervingly to date. The list soon became widely popular in libraries having dictionary catalogues in USA and abroad. Being a standard model, American bias in selection of preferred headings, terminology and spellings used had little effect on its contagious popularity abroad. Underneath its acceptability lies its responsiveness to users needs and technical advances in information science. Its 2nd (1926) and 3rd (1933) editions were brought again by Sears herself who died prematurely at the age of sixty. The 4th (1926) and 5th (1944) edition brought out by Isabel Stevenson Monro toed the line set by the founder. The Sixth edition (1950), edited by Bertha M. Frick, incorporated Sears name in the title and dropped the qualifier for small libraries to acquire its present title: Sears *List of Subject Headings*, as by this time it had also made its forays into medium size libraries. It become a reigning and standard tool for small as well as medium type libraries and acquired a stable format of internal codified instructions for vocabulary control, syndetic relations, and cross references in the list and for public catalogues. This format lasted till the 14th edition (1991). The abridged DDC numbers which were given for the first time to the headings in the 4th edition (1939) were dropped in the 9th edition (1965) with the plea that they were not being used for the purpose they were given; these were taken not as guide but substitute for the DDC schedules. The DDC numbers appeared again in the 11th edition following wide criticism from the body of users. Now the DDC numbers seem to stay put.

The orientation to the online environment started with the 13th edition (1986) edition jointly by Carmen Rovira and Caroline Reyes. It was the first edition to be created as an online database for editorial use. More than that it initiated some changes to suit online database searches and OPACs by transcribing headings in natural form : most of the preferred headings were deinverted *i.e.* straightened to go with the changed approach of users in search of electronic information. It also eased congestion of entries under a single entry word. *For example,* all entries pertaining to libraries got scattered by the initial word instead of all converging under the word "library" *i.e.* public libraries will file under P, and school libraries under "S". Since this edition (13th) ALA Filing Rules (1980) are being followed for arrangement of entries in the *List*.

New headings were mainly included from the area such as health and environment, computer science, space technology, changing family relations, minorities, consumerism, business and management.

More than this, on the suggestions of the Cataloguing of Children's Material Committee of ALA headings from the LC *Subject Headings for Children's Literature* are incorporated since the 13th edition. Therefore, Sears since then is also useful for children material. With the creation of electronic database the revisions became frequent and short spaced in time to keep it uptodate with new knowledge, terminology and subject heading techniques.

In the 15th edition (1994) edited by Dr. Joseph Miller the deinversion of headings was completed except for "State", The" and names of battles. *For example*, the previous heading "Art, Islamic" became Islamic art, and so with all such headings. It was believed that majority of the users search a subject in an electronic database under its natural form of the name. It is a major variation from the LC practice. In the 15th edition about 500 headings were modified or newly added. About 120 new headings were added to provide subject and genre access to individual works of fiction, drama, poetry and other imaginative works of films and television, *e.g.* Didactic drama, Horror films, Medical novels, and Science fiction, Television programmes. The milestone change since the Sears-15 is the thesaurus format display of headings and their relations using standard thesaural abbreviations NT, BT, RT, UF, USE and SA instead of x, xx and 'see also' for codified instructions. The thesaurus format conforms to the NISO standards for thesaurus (1993). Nevertheless, Sears remains a list instead of a true thesaurus. Only the relations amongst headings are now more explicitly visible, though the display of headings and cross references in the public catalogue remains the same. *For example*,

Forensic sciences 363.25

Use of materials on science as applied in courts of law or in criminal investigations

UF Criminalistics, Forensic science

BT Science

NT Medical jurisprudence

RT Criminal investigation

In the above entry the headings against UF, *i.e.*, used for are non-preferred headings for which cross references from these headings will be prepared leading to Forensic science for the public catalogue, *i.e.*

Criminalistics
See Forensic sciences
Forensic Science
See Forensic sciences

For BT, RT, NT, we may prepare see also downward references from BT to NT, *viz.*,

Science
See also Forensic sciences
Forensic sciences
See also Medical jurisprudence

While for RT, which links related headings or headings of equal specificity, making of *see also* references though optional, is permissible both ways

Criminal investigation
See also Forensic sciences
Forensic sciences
See also Criminal investigation

In the 16th edition (1997), the second one edited by Joseph Miller, the process of reformulating the headings in tune with the literary warrant and users approach to the subject indexes has taken a step further. The latest edition lists 7196 established headings of subjects including 55 personal, 68 corporate names, and 38 uniform titles. There are total of 7043 topical headings including a few geographic names given as key (model) headings. It includes all changes made in the annual electronic updates since the Sears-15 (1994) and contains 28 pages more of the core list over the previous edition. The revision of headings, as usual, is based on suggestions from Sears users, commercial bibliographic services vendors, and mostly from the staff of the H.W. Wilson Company engaged in cataloguing and indexing for their various products and services. The updated *Library of Congress Subject Headings* is always consulted. In the Sears-16 some headings are new for newly added subjects while some old subjects have acquired new terminology; and some of the terms have acquired new structure or grammar. Some of the newly added headings are in the field of computer science and engineering, such as Computer simulation, Hypertext, HTML, Multimedia systems, and World Wide Web. Other important new additions include Big bang theory, Physical fitness centres and Forest conservation. There are 316 such new subject headings.

Some headings have been changed or modified terminologically to reflect current usage. Long list of such headings has been provided (on pages xlvii-li) to highlight the differences between the immediate previous and present editions. Inside the List such changes between these two editions are indicated by a formal note:

Police brutality (May subdiv. geog.) 363.2
UF Police – complaints against [*Former heading*]
  Police cruelty
  Police repression
  Police violence
BT Police

These include new wordings, *e.g.* Xerography has at last been replaced by photocopying, space ships has been replaced by space vehicles. Changes may be in punctuation marks: X-rays replaces X = rays. A singular noun may be changed to a plural to *vice versa*: CD-ROM has been replaced by CD-ROMs; but Upper classes by Upper class. Some of the compound headings have been structured as subdivided headings: Religion–Biography replaces Religious biography. As another change: Birds-Eggs and nests has been reduced to two headings: Birds-Eggs; Birds-Nests. There are numerous such assorted changes. A commendable and epoch-making feature is the reduction of Christian bias. *For example*, Doctrinal theology which connotated Christian doctrine in the previous edition now connoted fundamental theology in general as evident from the suggested DDC numbers 230; 291.2, whereas in the previous edition only 230 was suggested. This has been done mostly by revising the scope and relations of the headings than by changing the headings themselves. *For example*:

Sears-16		Sears-15	
Doctrinal theology 230; 291.2		*Doctrinal theology* 230	
UF	Dogmatic theology Dogmatics Fundamental theology Systematics theology Theology, doctrinal [*Former heading*]	UF	Christian doctrine Dogmatic theology Dogmatics Theology, Doctrinal [*Former heading*]
SA	names of religion or Denominations with The subdivision *Doctrines, e.g. Christianity*-Doctrines... To be added as needed	BT	Theology
		NT	Liberation theology Love (Theology) Regeneration (Theology) Salvation Trinity
BT	Theology		
NT	Christianity-Doctrines Creeds Grace (Theology) Judaism-Doctrines Man (Theology) Salvation		

Some new commonly used subdivision have also been added. For every subdivision there is now an entry point in the core list and a note with instructions on the application of that subdivision. There are 204 such general references records. *For example*, Genetic aspects appears in the list of *Commonly used subdivisions* (page xlii) and also on page 314 of Sears-16:

Genetic aspects
Use type of diseases with the subdivision

Genetic aspects, *e.g.* Cancer-Genetic aspects; to be added as needed.

It simply means that the subject headings and their commonly used subdivisions are integrated in a cumulative way; the notes in the core list specify the area of applications of the subdivisions which are not universally applicable. In fact such an integration makes the separated list of commonly used subdivisions (pp. xli-xliii) somewhat redundant or simply of theoretical value. Their inclusion in the core list provides specific guidance on their application. It is more profitable to take these common subdivisions from the main list than from its separate list.

Another noteworthy change lies in the Key headings for places. In the Sears-15 and before, in some cases, the place names (of countries, states, cities) were the subject headings subdivided by the topic or subject. *For example*, *Chicago(Ill.)–Industries*. In the Sears-16 it has been replaced by *Industries–Chicago (Ill)*. Seven headings pertaining to a city have been so reversed. There is reversal of eight headings under Ohio, *e.g.* Ohio– Constitution has been replaced by Constitution–Ohio. Fourteen headings for the US have been affected so, *e.g.*, United States-Civil defence has been replaced by Civil defence- United States; United States–Diplomatic and consular service has been replaced by American diplomatic and consular services. Another change in case of geographic subdivision is the eradication of the adjectival form for a geographic subdivision of a topic. Now all geographic subdivisions are shown by a dash whereas in previous to Sears-15 some geographic subdivision of a topic were indicated by a comma. *For example* Folk art, American (Sears-14) (1991) is now *American Folk Art*.

Changes in the commonly used subdivisions are numerous. Following is the list of newly added subdivisions in the Sears-16.

Air conditioning
Comic books
Computer simulation
Conduct of life
Criticism
Death
Dental care
Diaries
Drug testing
Drying
Dwellings
Ecology
Editing
Employees
Ethical aspects
Ethics
Evaluation
Evolution
Explorations
Food
Forecasting
Foreign influence
Genealogy
Influence
Information Services
Library resources
Life cycles
Life skill guides
Literary collections
Manuscripts
Medical examinations
Mental health
Monuments
Nursing
Obituaries
Parodies, imitations, etc.
Pensions
Personal finance
Personal narratives
Physiological aspects
Physiology
Planning
Political aspects
Posters
Prayers
Rates
Rites and ceremonies
Scholarships
Specifications
Treatment
War use
Waste disposal
Wounds and injuries

It may be added that these are not new to the list. Some of them were provided in the Sears-15 and have been included in the list of commonly used subdivisions. Following Subdivisions have been deleted:

Contracts and specifications

Desertions	Pattern
Entrance requirements	Photography from space
Fire and fire prevention	Practice
Heating and ventilations	Professional ethics
Home care	Recruiting
Inservice training	Segregation
Integration	Thermodynamics
Inspection	Tournaments
Medals, badges...	Toxicology
Music	Transplantation

Some of these commonly used subdivisions have been transferred to the main body of the SHs. Some of the commonly used subdivisions have been modified:

Kings, queens, rulers, etc. has been replaced by Kings and rulers; Moral and religious aspects has been replaced by two new subdivisions: Ethical aspects, and Religious aspects. This makes it possible to have a heading like Ethnic relations–Religious aspects. Safety appliances replaces safety devices; and, Travel replaces Voyages and travels.

Number of headings having scope notes has increased. Clear and copious scope notes, resulting in improved presentation of information in the *List*, are another commendable feature of the new edition. Scope notes have also been added to identify any heading that may be assigned to individual works of drama, fiction, poetry, etc. *For example*, Easter-Drama; Lincoln, Abraham-Fiction.

DDC numbers from the Abridged 13th edition (1997) have been given as suggested numbers. A class number only exceptionally exceeds four or five digits unless it is extended by Area Table 2, *e.g.* United States–Rural conditions 307.720973. Only occasionally a number may exceed the average limit, *e.g. Popular music–Texts* 782.42164; Intellectual co-operation 327.1; 370.116. Some headings such as Charters, Exhibitions, Gifts, National characteristics have not been given DDC numbers on the plea that these "cannot be classified unless a specific application is identified". These headings could have been given an interdisciplinary number as has been done in the case of Directories 910.25.

The Sears-16 strengthens and continues the policies and consolidates the reforms set in by Sears-15; and still is a living manifestation of the principles of subject cataloguing put forth by C A Cutter (1837-1903) a century ago in his famous *Rules for a Dictionary Catalogue*. The Sears-16 is quite practical keeping in view the current needs and users behaviour in consulting the subject catalogues in OPACs. Its terminology is uptodate and international. However, some decisions regarding whether a place name be made a heading or a subdivision in some cases can be debated.

Printing and production standards are high, though margins on each side of the page are inadequate to record decisions and incorporate locally coined headings. There seems no use of repeating on every page the full forms of standard thesaural legends BT, RT, NT, SA, and UF when once these have been explained on page lii-facing page 1. The editors may also consider restoring the one page highly concise operational manual discontinued since the tenth edition.

The new edition brings in many changes in a short span of time. It is manifestation of its commitment and eagerness to keep itself uptodate on the knowledge front, terminologically and technically. Within a span of 75 years and fifteen revisions it has added 4000 new headings over the initial beginning of 3202 headings in 1923. It means the growth rate of 52 headings a year, or 266 headings per edition, Its skill lies in judiciously controlling the growth of the list in face of turbulently growing knowledge. Consistently the latest knowhow from information science has been developed to modernise internal structure and grammar of the list. This policy and urge accounts for its acceptability and popularity. Sears is an A-class product from a World class organization with avon editorial machinery. It has no rival. It sets its own challenges and meets them; and thus has an assured foreseeable future.

Sears List of Subjects Headings –16th ed/ed. By Joseph Miller. New York; Ohio: The H.W. Wilson Company, 1997. Lii, 786 p. ISBN 0-8242-0920-6.

APPENDIX

A CHRONOLOGY OF THE SEARS LIST OF SHs

Edition	Year	Editor	Salient features/main changes
1.	1923	Minnie Earl Sears	List of subject headings for small libraries: compiled from lists used in nine representatives small libraries. Contains only "See" and corresponding refer from headings.
2.	1926	"	Quite enlarged. "See also" references added.
3.	1933	"	A chapter on "Practical suggestions for the beginners in the subject headings work added. List of commonly used subdivisions added separately.
4.	1939	Isabel Stevenson Monro	DDC numbers added to the headings based on the usage in the H. W. Wilson standard catalogues. Subtitle dropped. Subdivisions of general applications were printed in italics. Number of headings 3870.
5.	1944	"	–
6.	1950	Bertha M. Frick	Incorporated Sears' name and dropped the qualifier "for small libraries" to assume the present title. The "see" and "refer from" instructions were replaced by x and xx symbols to conform to the LCSH 5th ed (1948).
7.	1954	"	–
8.	1959	"	Number of headings 4614
9.	1965	Barbara M. Westby	DDC numbers omitted. New headings added chiefly from science and technology field.
10.	1972	"	Number of headings 5326. New headings added from social and environmental protection.
11.	1977	"	DDC numbers restored. Chapter on practical suggestions revised to be renamed as "Principles of the Sears list of subject headings". Terms neutralised by removing gender and racial bias. Section on non-book material added in the Principles.

Edition	Year	Editor	Salient features/main changes
12.	1982	Barbara M. Westby	Subject headings for children's literature from LC merged with Sears.
13.	1986	Carmen Rovira and Caroline Reyes	Filing order based on ALA filing rules 1980 with some modifications. Deinversion of headings started. Both the changings were necessary to facilitate computerised searches. Class numbers from DDC-11 and 12 added.
14.	1991	Martha T Mooney	Revision reforms continued in line with the use of computers. Many number of compound headings reduced to simple ones.
15.	1994	Josoph Miller	"Principles of Sears list of subject headings" revised. Thesaurus format introduced and deinversion of headings almost completed. List of cancelled and replaced headings added.
16.	1997	"	Consolidates the changes of Sears 15. Christian bias reduced.

2

CONTROLLED VOCABULARY

Definition, Need and Purpose, Tools

Language is the key to all information retrieval. Every unit of discrete information must be analysed, given a suitable descriptor, which is labelled either on the item or on its surrogates and placed in the information storage system for efficient and reliable retrieval. For subject access (as distinguished from author, title and other approaches) these labels are termed as subject descriptors; and obviously must be based on the subject contents of the documents. These subject descriptors constitute what is known as an *subject indexing language.*

These descriptors are usually based upon two types of languages :

1. Artificial shorthand or coded language based on some ordinal symbols/digits called notation. *For example* 954 or V44 for History of India in the Dewey Decimal Classification, and Colon Classification respectively. Such a coded symbol, essentially based on a notational system, is called a class number and are used for arrangement of information bearing items in the information store. These numbers may also be used for arrangement of entries in a catalogue or bibliography. This approach is very logical, almost systematic, but highly contrived. S R Ranganathan calls it an artificial language of ordinal digits.

Problems

For the ordinary and uninitiated users it has to be learnt

diligently to effectively retrieve the information from the store. Therefore, expectedly, it cannot be easily and thoroughly used by the majority of the users. Users have to be educated even for its shallow use. It essentially needs an alphabetical index for its full and effective use even by the trained librarians. That is why it has been very aptly said that natural language provides the ultimate key to all information retrieval systems. Since the class numbers are assigned to the documents for their arrangement in the information store, so for retrieval of a particular document we will have to use the pre-assigned class number as such. Therefore, such a language is called *pre-coordinated indexing language.*

A C Foskett terms such systems as one place indexes as "they give a place which we consider to be the primary statement of the subject, though they may need supporting secondary listing in a different order to give full access".* Since such descriptors are assigned using a language taken from outside sources such languages are also known as *assigned descriptors.*

2. *Natural Language Descriptors*

Second type of indexing languages use descriptors from natural languages words to avoid the problems posed by artificial indexing languages. Natural language descriptors are of two types (a) Free and uncontrolled language, (b) Controlled language.

Free Language

It is also known as uncontrolled or freetext indexing language. A freetext descriptor is taken from the ordinary and unmanipulated language as it appears in the document. It may be taken from the title, book blurbs, table of contents, annotations or key words as given by the author,

---

* A. C. Foskett. *The subject Approach to Information* 5th ed. London: The Library Association Publishing, 1996, p. 213

Descriptors without any contrivance may be taken from any of these sources. Advantage of such descriptors is that these are simple, current, easy to use and totally inexpensive. It does not require any expertise in using or maintaining such an indexing language. No authority list is required for this purpose.

Disadvantages of Freetext Indexing

To count disadvantages, such a language is full of homonyms, synonyms, using different spellings for some words and a word being used in different senses and shades of meanings. *For example*, Tsar or Czar; Renaissance or Renascence; labor, though having different spellings have the same meaning. Similarly pay, salary, wages, remuneration, are synonymous or near synonymous terms. As another example, staff, workers, employees, workforce, human resources, personnels, establishment are used interchangeably. Bridge is a game and an engineering structure; cricket is an insect and a popular game. The word pitch has many meanings. Brian and Alina Vickery point out that 20 most frequently used English nouns have an average of seven meanings.* The word "order" has about 250 meanings in the Oxford English Dictionary. It will be a librarians utopia if there were one to one relationship between concepts and terms. In reality there are cultural and dialectical variations within a language besides many shades of meanings; and there are always some people who prefer to call a spade by some other name. Ordinary language has jargon, slang, literary and dialectic differences between different sectors and strata of people in the society. Teenagers develop their own words and word usages. British English differs markedly from American English. Indian English has its own vocabulary even idioms. In nutshell a language is totally ingrained in the social fabric and changes as the society changes with place and time.

---

* Quoted by A C Foskett *op. cit.*, p. 80.

Then there are many written variants of a word *e.g.* Three Dimensions, 3D or 3-D;UN or United Nations; Text book, Text-book or Textbook. There is always a question of scientific and ordinary names. Should we use:

Cat or *Felis domesticus*
Potato or *Solanum tuberosum*

Iron or *Ferrous*
Flowering Plants or *Cryptogamia*
Child diseases or *Paediatrics*

The natural language that we use is at the same time varied, rich, deep, shallow, playful, exciting dull, boring, unemotive, poor and inadequate to exactly express thoughts and feelings. It is artistic and legalistic, poetic and prosaic, beautiful and uncouth; ambiguous and perspicuous; abundant, redundant and inadequate. Its variants and nuances are many. Poets, fiction writers, playwrights and other men of letters bank on this innate quality of the language which in turn conveys the moods, ideas, feelings, emotions and experiences of the writer. Ordinary language is both the best tool of communication as well as a barrier in communication. It is both deceptive and vague; apt and succinct. It is at best an imperfect tool of communication. But no other tool is better than this.* It can be largely cured of its imperfections.

Therefore, if such a free language is used as an indexing language the information in the store will get scattered. Some information will get indexed under *wages*; some other under *pay*; another chunk under *salary*, and so on. A user will have to search under all these terms for a complete recall of information on this topic. Even if a user knows all these descriptions she will be taking much time to search under all these terms. It means it is time taking.

---

* S R Ranganathan : Prolegemena to library classification 3rd ed (1967). Bangalore: Sarada Ranganathan Endowment, 1989 (reprint) chapter GA.

But the greater problem is that a user may not know of all the descriptors used for a given concept. So in the store the information may remain buried under different labels. It will considerably decrease the recall ratio of the system *i.e.,* only a fraction of the relevant documents will get retrieved.

On the other hand if the descriptors are used without distinction or precision (*i.e.* descriptor terms are 'homonymous or vague) the search may yield some irrelevant documents. *For example*, under the term cricket one will get information both on the game and the insect which may unlikely be of interest to a single user. In brief, the use of free language as indexing language will result in low recall and low precision. Hence, ultimately it will prove to be very costly. To make up for the deficiencies of a natural language as a subject indexing language we need a bit controlled language. Thus, the use of controlled vocabulary for subject description is pretty obvious. Computer aided information retrieval (CAIR) has even enhanced the usefulness of a controlled vocabulary. Boolean logic used with freetext searching produces many false drops (irrelevant information). Database searching needs unified terminology.

We need to make our systems more efficient, though designing operating and maintaining such an information storage and retrieval system is a costly affair. But like cheap education we never stop paying for a cheap indexing system. Despite the problem of consensus and other barriers the work of achieving control over terms used as subject descriptors is essential and useful.

Controlled Vocabulary

Therefore, there should be some control on the vocabulary that we use as descriptors for alphabetical subject indexing– though the descriptors are derived from a natural language. This is called standardized terminology. This control is twofold:

(a) It has select vocabulary: out of the many terms for a given concept only one term is selected as index term/descriptor/ subject heading. There should always be one to one correspondence between the concept and the term denoting it. That is, a concept should be denoted by one and only one term and *vice versa.* Out of the many candidate terms for a given concept the selected term is known as preferred term. "See" cross reference is provided from each of the non-preferred term to the preferred/used term. It has its own grammar.

(b) Controlled vocabulary is not simply a reservoir of select terms. It is a system of terms. It has its own grammar *i.e.* structure of headings in case of multiworded headings; definite rules about the use of singular or plural form; rules and punctuations for synthesis of terms; and explicit depiction of relations with other terms falling in that class. A standard authority list will allow the use of only one of the followings: Bird Photography, photographing birds; Photography and Birds, Photography, Birds, Birds–Photography.

A controlled vocabulary is thus an objective means to reduce variety and playfulness of ordinary language. It is an instrument of indexing for maximum recall amenable to predictable pattern. We only gain in search efficiency at the cost of increased input time and expenses. Controlled vocabulary has many advantages of classification with notation *sans* its disadvantages.

Standard Authority Lists

To provide controlled "indexing vocabulary for an ISAR system we can either frame specific rules as C A Cutter

(1837-1903) did in his famous *Rules for a Dictionary Catalogue* (1876); or there can be a standardised procedure for coining index terms such as Precis, Popsi, Chain indexing, Compass, or Nephis. These are set of established procedure for a pre-coordinated string of terms in which each term is semantically defined and syntactically related to hierarchial, synonyms and related terms.

On the other hand there are standard sources, such as lists of subject headings and thesauri which list readymade index terms and provide rules for combination of terms both at the input and search stages. These in fact provide complete guidance in designing subject catalogues. Such tools are easy to operate, though not that easy to design, and are meant both for the cataloguer and the end user. That is, these are not only helpful for the purpose of assigning subject headings/descriptor labels to document surrogates by the cataloguers, but are equally essential for the end users to formulate, modify or negotiate searches by the user as the enquiry proceeds. Some of the outstanding examples are:

Library of Congress Subject Headings
4 Vols. 1990 –

Canadian Subject Headings. National Library of Canada

Subject headings for school and public libraries 2nd ed/Joanna F. Fountain. Littleton, Colo. : Libraries Unlimited, 1996

Subject Headings for Children : A List of subject Headings Used by the Library of Congress with Dewey Numbers added. 2 vols. 2nd ed. Albany, NY : Forest Press, 1997.

Medical Subject Headings, (MeSH)/ by National Library of Medicine (USA)

Subject headings for African American materials by

Lorene B Brown. Littleton : Libraries Unlimited, 1995.

Sears List of Subject Headings. HW Wilson, 1923-

Art and Architecture Thesaurus New York : Oxford University Press, 1990-1992. 3 vols.

There are numerous thesauri both at the international and local levels. Now subject headings lists are also being designed in thesaurus format. A Subject heading list is a precoordinated indexing language while a thesaurus is a tool for post coordinated indexing language. Thesauri began to appear and proliferate in the mid-twentieth century. A thesaurus shows relations between indexing terms more vividly and explicitly, thus, it is a classification tool with a greater number of systematic features than a traditional shelf classification. It is usually intended for use in a machine readable database of a narrow subject area. And is called a machine language sometimes.

In a standard list of subject headings (SHs)

(a) SHs are explicitly listed, usually alphabetically.

(b) Some of the preferred headings can be further divided by topics, forms, or by geographical and chronological subdivisions.

(c) Guidance is provided for coining of required SHs on the pattern of some model or key headings.

(d) Instructions are given at places to coin specific headings than a given heading belonging to class *e.g.* under dogs we are instructed to coin 'Alsations' etc., if needed.

(e) Provides inbuilt guidance in the choice of right headings in a maze of synonyms scattered alphabetically; in other words lead is provided to the preferred headings from non-preferred headings.

Thus, a standard list helps to coin far more SHs than merely listed; and provides guidance in designing subject catalogues, and a web of cross references for maximum recall and minimum of irrelevant retrievals. It is a complete system.

Summary

Our day to day language though the most powerful and most commonplace tool of communication is not as such, fit for scientific and precise communication. Language is also the ultimate indexing tool. When used as such in raw form without any manipulation or control it is called freetext. Freetext indexing language not being efficient in information retrieval, we need controlled vocabulary wherein terms are highly select and have its own grammar. For vocabulary control there may either be a procedural systems such as Cutter's Rule, Precis, Popsi, Chain indexing and suchlike systems, or there may be standard authority lists. The Sears List of Subject Heading is one such authority list which is a reservoir of enumerated SHs, and provides models and guidance for constructing many more SHs on the pattern of key headings and categories of omitted SHs. It also provides guidance in designing of subject catalogues.

Exercise

1. Why is a indexing language needed for information retrieval?
2. What is a freetext indexing language? List its problems.
3. Define a standard authority list? Name a few authority lists.

3

PRINCIPLES OF THE SEARS LIST

Every system of controlled vocabulary is based on some principles regarding

* Choice of preferred headings
* Levels of specificity
* Form and structure of headings

These issues constitute the principles of the system and the grammar of the headings. Grammar is based on linguistic principles. Their choice and structure is determined by thinking in the information science, advances in users studies, and the literary warrant *i.e.* usage of terms in the currently published literature. The **Sears List**, since its beginning is based on some definite and clearly stated principles. These principles, though mostly based on the Library of Congress Subject Headings, have been modified to suit its target libraries – that is, small and medium type libraries.* These principles in turn can be traced back to the principles of subject cataloguing laid down by C A Cutter (1837-1903) in his famous *Rules for a Dictionary Catalogue* (1873, 3rd ed. 1903). These clearly stated rules for subject catalouging are:

1. Direct and specific entry
2. Common usage
3. Uniformity and consistency

* Obviously the target users, hence the levels of both these lists are different. The *Sears* is meant for small and medium type libraries, while the *LCSH* aims at the big and research libraries. The Sears is shorter in size; number of headings and there subdivisions is less detailed. In the Sears comparatively the headings are less complex and less specific.

All these principles are quite common but not quite unambiguous : to some extent these principles are relative and subjective. Nevertheless these have been sufficiently explained and illustrated in chapter "Principles...." (pp xvi-xviii) Sears-16 and in other numerous writings on subject indexing.

1. Direct and Specific Entry

This principle lays down that a subject be entered directly under its own specific name rather than under the class to which it belongs. "Specific" means exact and succinct term corresponding to the subject of the document, *i.e.,* the term should be an exact measure of the depth and breadth of the subject. In other words the heading should be as specific as possible. *For example,* "Rose" is to be entered under the heading "Rose" rather than under the class "Flowers". A dog is entered under "dogs" rather than the class "Domestic Animals" or under "Mammals". As another example, a book say on the life of Charles Darwin, will be entered under his name Darwin, Charles, and not under the heading "Scientists" or even "Naturalists". As another example subject heading for Alsatians, is Alsatians, not Dogs. Similarly a document on Thermodynamics is given the heading "Thermodynamics" not heat, or physics. *

Direct Entry

It means specific heading should be the lead heading, instead of a subdivisions. *For example,* Water birds–Penguins is a specific entry, but only *Penguins* is a direct and specific entry. Similarly Civil Engineering–Bridges, or even

---

* But this specificity is not something absolute. It may be subjective and at best depends upon the largeness and specialisation of the library collection/database, and of course on the level of users. More and more specificity may be required as the collection grows. *For example* Library of Congress subject headings are more specific than sears headings; while MeSH is more specific and detailed than the Library of Congress SHs.

Civil Engineering–Transportation–Bridges is specific entry, but Bridges is both specific and direct. Even "Suspension bridges" is entered under this heading instead of Bridges–Suspension bridges. Latter is known as alphabetic-classed catalogue. An alphabetic-classed catalogue has an advantage of collecting entries on a given topic with its subordinate headings. In a dictionary catalogue direct entries are convenient and time saving.**

Another ambiguity lies in the level of specification, *viz.,* How much specific a catalogue should be. *For example,* should we use the term "Retina" or dump it under "Eye". Should we use the term *Thrombosis* or enter it under Heart. The answer of course is subjective and depends upon local conditions of a given library and its policy. *For example, Thrombosis* will be entered under "*heart*" in a small or general library. But in a medical library it will be entered under *Thrombosis*.

Common Usage

Sears adheres to the principle of common usage (both with regard to terms chosen as preferred headings and spellings). It uses common and popular terms instead of scientific or technical terms or jargon. On other words it uses terminology current among majority of lay users: "A General rule is to use a popular or common rather than a scientific or technical term where there is a choice" (Sears-16, p. xvii).

** A disadvantage of direct entry is that the material on a given topic will get scattered under even minute headings pertaining to a specific class. *For example*, information, say, on dogs will get scattered under headings Terriers, Hounds, Collies, German shepherds, Alsatians, Guide dogs, and so on. Of course some material will get entered under the heading Dogs. For such a catalogue it will be time taking, if not difficult to find out total number of entries on dogs. Moreover the users will have to be directed through the maze of *see also* entries for an exhaustive search on dogs. *For example* the catalogue entry on dogs must refer the users to kinds and species of dogs, and under colliies it must also refer to Teerriers and other breeds.

For example, Sears uses "Dinners" instead of "Banquets", "Film festivals" instead of "Motion picture festivals"; "Pseudonyms" instead of "Fictitious names", "Airplanes" instead of "Aeroplanes"; "Elderly" instead of "Aged"; Birds instead of "Orinthology".

Regarding spellings a subject headings list has to settle, once for all, between color and colour, labor and labour; Czar and Tsar; Renascence and Renaissance. Sears no doubt uses American terms and spellings. Libraries outside America can make corresponding alterations especially in case of spellings. A library must adhere to the tradition and culture of its country.

Common usage is not easily determinable. Besides this, it also changes with time. *For example*, Linguistics was once popularly called Philology; Economics was known as Political economy; Library science was library economy in good old days. Even at given time the current usage may differ from class to class of users, and from country to country even from place to place. In a science library "Aves" may be preferred over Birds. In a medical library Paediatrics is the term for child diseases. Conventional advice is: employ humane, non-pejorative nomenclature favoured by the concerned group. *For example* use "Blacks" instead of Negroes; Hansen's Disease instead of Leprosy.

Uniformity. This is an obvious principle, rather the very reason for compiling such lists. It means:

(a) That a heading once used should be consistently and uniformly be applied in its scope and meaning until a decision is taken to the contrary.

(b) Singular, plural forms be used consistently– based on some objectively stated criteria.

(c) Spellings once chosen be used uniformly.

Grammar and Structure of Subject Headings

Uniformity in subject headings is achieved by strictly laying down explicit and unambiguous rules for singular or plural form of a term; word order in a phrasal or multiworded term, and structure of heading having subdivision(s). Sears rules are enumerated below:

Single Noun Headings

Many of he headings in the Sears are simply of single noun either in singular or plural form *e.g.* Actors, Africa, Birds, Carbon, Comedies, Comedy, Jungles, Soils, Songs, Yoga, Zoology.

Singular nouns are:

Abstract nouns	:	Bravery, Truth, Credit, War
Broad areas of knowledge	:	Chemistry, Political Science, Education, Poetry, Physics
Plural nouns are	:	Concrete countable objects: Books, Rocks, Crystals, Fables, Storms, Whales

Plural noun is considered more common.

The broader rule is: How much is expressed in singular; how many in plural form.

But the judgement to apply this rule is not simple. In some cases both the singular and plural forms are used, which of course have different meanings. *For example*, Theater denotes drama as acted on the stage while Theatres denote theatre buildings. Essay means a genre or technique of writing essays; whereas Essays denotes a literary form, *e.g.* a collection of essays. Similarly, symphony is a musical form; symphonies mean musical scores.

In some cases there is a guidance whether a particular class of headings to be formed should be in singular or plural form. *For example,* under:

Trees (may sub. div.geog)

SA types of trees *e.g. Oak*, to be added
as needed in a *singular form*. [Emphasis added]
For example, Apple, Lemon, Oak, Mango.

The following useful guide has been taken from A C Foskett (*op cit p.* 79) regarding the choice of singular or plural forms.

Type of term	*Use Singular*	*Use Plural*
Material Properties	When specific, *e.g.* Polythene Density	When generic, *e.g.* Plastics Chemical properties
Objects Events Objectives specified by purpose		Cars Laws Wars Lubricant
Processes Proper names Disciplines Subject areas	Lubricating Earth (the planet) Law War	

Synonyms

In case of synonyms a parenthetical qualifier is used to define the context. Lime (Fruit); Lime (Mineral). Ice; Ice (Drug). Depression (Psychology), Depression–latter is used for economic depressions. Some more examples are: Ensembles (Music), Earthwork (Art). A free heading without qualifier is usually reserved for common and popular usage. In case of equal usage both such words are qualified: Lime (Fruit); Lime (Mineral).

Phrase Headings

Some complex subjects can only be described appropriately by a phrase in a pre-coordinated index. Phrase headings are coined with less certainly of their uniformity or acceptability. These are of three kinds:

1. Having a conjunction "and" *i.e.* in the form noun

and noun

2. Adjectival heading *i.e.* Adjective and noun.
3. Prepositional phrase headings

Noun and noun headings are joined together by "and". These put together two related or opposite concepts:

Libraries and students
Collectors and collecting
Arts and craft movement
Banks and banking
Design and constructions
Wine and wine making
Communism and religion
Open and closed shops
Voyages and travels
Rites and ceremonies
Weights and measures

2. Adjectival nouns

All the former inverted headings have now been put in Adjective and noun order. Most of the phrasal headings in the *List* belong to this category. *For example:*

Arab civilization
Economic policy
Portable computers
Urban sociology
Geographic names
American fiction
Bible fiction
English fiction
Religious fiction
Love stories
Ground effect machines
Glow in the dark books
International ballistic missiles
New Age Movement

North Atlantic Treaty Organization

As said earlier, prior to Sears–15 most of these headings were inverted to bring noun in the front position to collocate a subject with all its kinds:

Chemistry, Inorganic
Chemistry, Organic
Chemistry, Physical

But in the age of OPACs the natural forms have been found more useful.

Prepositional Phrased Headings

Some complex concepts are expressed by nouns or noun phrases connected by prepositions

Picture books for children
Applications for positions
Library of Congress
Right to die
Life on other planets
Artificial satellites in telecommunication
Sexual behaviour in animals
Missions in action
Radio in education
Minorities in television
Meals on wheels programmes
Human influence on nature
Monasticism and religious orders for women
Social work with the elderly
Space flight to the moon
American prisoners of war

All these compound headings denoting complex concepts are based on literary warrant; and rules for coining such headings are based on National Information Standards Organisation (NISO) standards for thesaurus construction.

Subdivisions of Headings

Any of the preferred heading in the Sears List may be divided in three ways:

a. Topical subdivisions
b. Geographical subdivisions
c. Commonly used subdivisions

Some of the headings are already divided by some topical subdivisions *i.e.* subdivisions which are special to a given heading– *i.e.* these are aspects appropriate or unique to that heading.

Bible–Parables
Food–Fibre content
Dinosaurs–Eggs
Cancer–Chemotherapy
Buildings–Earthquake effect
Pianos–Tuning
Elderly–Institutional care
English language–Grammar
Photography–Developing and developers
Statistics–Graphic methods

There are many more such examples of topical subdivisions which are of course based on literary warrant.

Topical Subdivisions by instructions

Not all topical subdivisions are listed: some may be obtained by specific instructions given under a heading. *For example*:

Collective bargaining
May be subdivided by groups of professional or non-professional workers.

On this instruction we coin:

Collective bargaining – Nurses
Collective bargaining – Midwives
Collective bargaining – Teachers

Geographic subdivisions are obtained on instruction; or can be used on the pattern of the key geographic headings *United States*, *Ohio* and *Chicago* respectively. Commonly used subdivisions are applicable universally whenever needed. These types of subdivisions have been explained in the chapter exclusively devoted to "subdivisions."

Summary

Sears is based on the standard and long standing norms of coining subject headings, namely:

(a) Direct and specific entry

(b) Common usage

(c) Uniformity and consistency.

The principle of specific entry and common usage depends upon the strengths of collection, kind and level of users. Direct entry means a specified subject is to be entered directly rather than indirectly as a subdivision. *For example* "Alsatians" is entered as such instead of Dogs–Alsatians. Regarding common usage the choice has to be made whether to use Alsatians or German shepherds. Again the major deciding factor are the users – it should be common among the users. Headings are of two types : single nouns and phrasal headings. Single nouns are both singular and plural, *e.g.* Age, African, Canals, Gymnastics. Synonyms are distinguished by a qualifier *e.g.*, Ice; Ice (Drug). The rules regarding singular or plural use are clear : How much is singular; how many is plural. Multiworded or phrasal headings are of three types:

(a) Adjective nouns, *e.g.* Urban sociology

(b) Conjoined with "and" in the form noun and noun *e.g.* Banks and banking.

(c) Prepositional headings, which represent complex

concepts; Right to die; Life on other planets; Picture books for children.

A heading may be further subdivided either on instruction or of one's own; or it may be found subdivided in the list by an aspect – the latter is known as topical subdivision: *For example*: statistics–Graphic methods. A heading may also be subdivided topically on instruction. Two other important subdivisions of any heading are Commonly used subdivisions, and Geographical subdivisions.

Exercise

1. Name the three principles of the Sears List
2. Illustrate with examples the meaning of direct entry.
3. What is the basis for the use of singular or plural nouns used as headings? Give examples.
4. How many types of phrasal headings are in use in the Sears?
5. What is the device to differentiate the different meanings of a homonym?

4

STRUCTURE OF THE SEARS-16 (1997)

The Sears list is an alphabetical list of standard terms in English language spread to the whole gamut of knowledge intended for use in small and medium size libraries. The 16th edition of the list has the following bibliographical details:

> Sears, Minnie Earl: *Sears List of Subject Headings*,16th ed./edited by Joseph Miller. New York: The H.W. Wilson Company, 1997, lii, 786p. ISBN 0-8242-0920-6.

It may be deemed to consist of two parts: the introductory part whose pages are numbered by Roman numerals (ppi-lii); and the core list of subject headings proper whose pages are numbered by Indo-Arabic numerals (pp1-786). In the preliminary pages "Principles of Sears List" (pp xv-xxxxiii) is a clear, comprehensive but concise introduction to "what" and "how" of the Sears system. It is indeed an operational manual which explains with illustrations the purpose of subject cataloguing and the basic principles underlying the design of the list and the procedure to consult and use it. It serves as a brief manual to operate the list; to locate and coin or to adapt an appropriate headings; or to divide a heading further by commonly used subdivisions (pp xli-xliii) or as per instructions given under a particular heading. It is very practical in approach and should be read slowly and grasped fully. Editor's "Preface" (pp vii-xi) explains the history and scope of the Sears List and the process of its revision and updating. It may be noted that not all headings which can be minted from the list are enumerated. Many more can be self coined. Next important section named "Headings to be added by the cataloguer" (pp xxxix) is a list of 14 categories of headings (divided broadly into proper and common names), which have not been listed explicitly, but can be added by the cataloguers of their own: such headings are to be coined by cataloguers. Implied headings may by far outnumber the explicitly listed headings. Next follows the list of "Key" Headings (p. xl) which work as model subject headings for five types of headings pertaining to persons, peoples, places, languages and literatures, and wars. In the List one heading has been given as a model with subdivisions providing a pattern for coining analogous headings belonging to that class. *For example*, for language the English language (pp 254-56) with its subdivisions provides the pattern. On this analogy headings for any language and its aspects may be coined.

On pages xli-xliii is an alphabetical list of Commonly used subdivisions which can be used to subdivide any subject headings listed or otherwise obtained from the Sears List. Next chapter "Checking and Adding Headings" (pp xliv-xlv) provides practical tips for checking *i.e.* tick marking the headings used by the cataloguers. Also explained here is record keeping of any new or self coined headings used in a particular library. This also includes a "Simple Page of Checking" (p. xlv). These are practical tips for the bench cataloguers for maintaining and updating the subject authority file. Importance of such work has been explained in the section "Recording Headings and References" (p. xxxvii). Lastly there is an alphabetical "List of cancelled and Replacement Headings" (pp xlvii-li). The list mirrors changes in subject headings in this new edition. It is mostly useful to the libraries which were using the previous edition (15th, 1994) and now want to completely shift over to the new edition. It is a ready recokner for replacing the obsolete headings with the new and current ones. Complete guidance, however, for shifting over to the new edition from the old one has been given under the section "New Terminology for Existing Subjects" (pp xxxv-xxxvi). The several legends such as BT, RT, NT, UF, SA, and other abbreviated instructions under various entries have been fully spelled at page lvi, and also as footnotes on every page (pp 1-786) of the List *per se*. Full implications of these symbols for preparing cross references for the public catalogue have been explained at pages xxx-xxxiv under the heading "References".

Nature and structure of the List

The second part entitled Sears List of Subject Headings" (pp 1-786) is the *terra firma* of the system. This bicolumned list is to be referred to locate or coin appropriate subject heading(s) after subject analysis of the document. As said earlier, it is an alphabetical list, arranged word by word, of standard subject headings pertaining to the whole gamut of knowledge. Since the Sears-15 (1994), following the *Library of Congress Subjects Headings* the entries in the Sears have been given the format of a thesaurus, though it still remains basically a list of subject headings.

All the headings are of two types:

1. Non-preferred headings

Typographically such headings are printed in light type face. Being synonyms or other variants of a preferred heading, these are not used as headings:

For example:

3-D Photography
3 Mile limit
Abnormal children

Every page is full of such headings which could be a:

(a) Non-preferred synonym of a subject heading, *e.g.*

Law suits

Christian denominations
Insane

(b) an inverted form of the standard heading

Antiques, classical
Chemistry, organic

(c) different form of a heading

Jewish doctrines for Judaism-Doctrines

(d) Heading used in the previous edition

Jewish-Islamic relations

The category of non-preferred headings when listed under the preferred headings are stated as former heading, *e.g.*

Judaism-Relations-Islam
UF Islamic-Jewish relations
Jewish-Islamic relations [Former heading]

(e) different plural/singular or abbreviated form of a preferred heading

Laws for Law
3-D photography for *Three dimensional photography*
A.C.O.A.S. for *Adult children of Alcoholics*
A-bomb victims for *Atomic bomb victims*

(f) different spellings of a word

Labour
Color

(g) different lead component of a phrased heading:

Sociology and religion for Religion *and sociology*
Daughters and fathers for *Fathers and daughters*
Or any other variant of a used heading in the *List*.

All these non-preferred headings are invariably linked to the preferred heading by the directing word "USE" *e.g.*

Relations among ethnic groups
USE ***Ethnic relations***

Cardiac diseases
USE ***Heart diseases***

Obviously, the subject heading following the directing word "USE" is always in bold face. Interpreting the above entries it means that heading "Relations among ethnic group" and cardiac diseases are non-preferred headings and hence should not be used. Instead the cataloguer is at once directed at both these headings to use "Ethnic relations" and "Heart diseases" respectively given in bold type face. From these we go to these headings with full entity given in bold face at their alphabetical place in the list.

The usable or preferred forms of all the above headings are:

3-D photography
USE *Three dimensional photography*
3-mile limit
USE *Territorial waters*
Abnormal children
USE Exceptional children
Handicapped Children
Low suits
USE *Litigation*
Christian denominations
USE *Christian sects*
Antiques, classical
USE *Classical antiques*
Chronology, Biblical
USE *Bible-Chronology*
Church – Government policy
USE *Church and state*
Laws
USE *Law*

Legislation

Colour

Use *color* (in Indian context this will be reversed *i.e.* color

USE colour)

Sociology and religion

USE *Religion and sociology*

The cataloguers or the library users should never stop at the heading given against USE howsoever sure and proper heading it may appear to be. The cataloguers should instead revert to the directed preferred heading for two reasons:

(a) For verifications, though chances of error are rarest of rare.

(b) For full entry with DDC class number, scope note, instruction for subdivision, full listing of broader, narrower and related headings for making syndetic cross references. The full entry also provides instructions to add or coin appropriate apt and precise headings. Full entry helps the users in formulating search strategy. *For example*:

Dance (May subdiv. geog.) *792.8;793.3*

Use for materials on recreational dancing as well as performance dance

UF Dances
Dancing [Former heading]

SA types of dances and dancing, to be added as needed

BT *Amusements*
Performing arts

NT *Ballet*
Break dancing
Clog dancing

Folk dancing
Modern dancing
Tap dancing

RT *Aerobics*
Dance music

Against the bold face entry is given the instruction/permission that if needed this heading "may be subdivided geographically." In this case two examples of division by geographical area are given by way of illustrations. This is followed by the scope note "use of...". This note helps to know the definition and extension of the topic and tells about the kind of material that is to be accommodated under that heading. It explains in simple words the applications of the heading, and the type of reading material to which the heading is applicable. In other words it implies definition, limits of the headings, details about its application and may distinguish it from other closely related headings say Dance music. *For example.*

Electric apparatus and appliances 621.3028; 643
Use for materials...materials. On large machines powered by electricity are entered under *Electric machinery.*

There is a reciprocal note under *Electric machinery*

These legends and scope notes are quite important for fully understanding the entry and for preparing cross references for the public catalogue.

Summary

Used for vocabulary control the Sears List is an alphabetical list of standard subject headings arranged word by word order. In the preliminary part are given its history and revision process. Most important section of this part is the "Principles of Sears List of Subject Headings" which is a brief but complete operational manual. It explains the principles underlying its design and also provides guidance in locating, coining, synthesising even adapting subject headings in different situations. The second part "Sears List of Subject Headings" (pp 1-786) is the core part. The headings have been arranged in one alphabetical sequence and the structure is in thesaurus format based on ANSI/NISO Standards for thesauri (1993). There are two types of headings. Headings in light face are non-preferred headings which for various reasons are not used as SHs. These non-preferred headings invariably refer to the preferred headings by the legend USE. Preferred headings are always given in bold type face and contain full entry with scope note, instructions for subdivisions if any, alongwith depiction of BT, RT, NT headings. Headings for use should always be taken from the (main) preferred entry to carry out instructions and to prepare cross references for the public catalogue.

Exercise

1. Fully explain the arrangement of headings in the Sears List
2. Bring out the relations between preferred and non-preferred headings.
3. Give the structure of a standard (having all elements) preferred heading.

Domestic Relations 346.01
UF Family relations
BT Human relations
NT Desertion and nonsupport
Grandparents and child
Parents and child
Visitation rights (Domestic Relations)
RT Divorce
Family
Family life education
Marriage

Subject heading
always in bold face

Class number from
Abridged DDC-13

Make see cross reference
from this heading to
Domestic relations
i.e. Family relations
See domestic relations

Human Relations
See also Domestic relations

Domestic relation
See also
Desertion and nonsupport;
Grandparent and child;
Parent and child;
Visitation rights (Domestic
Relations).

Divorce *See also* Domestic relations.
Family *See also* Domestic relations.
Family life education
See also Domestic relations.
Marriage *See also* Domestic relations.

Domestic Relations
See also
Divorce;
Family;
Family life education;
marriage.

SYMBOLS

UF	Used For	RT	Related Term
BT	Broader Term	SA	See also
NT	Narrower Term		

Note : RT references are made on reciprocal basis

5

SUBJECT ANALYSIS

> "One of the fundamentals of cataloging is to use one's judgement based on the materials at hand and the purpose and the needs of the library"
>
> Sears-16, p. xxiv.

Process of assigning subject headings to a document is not different from assigning a class number to it. The aim of both is to provide subject approach to information. Classification provides it through the shelf arrangement of documents while subject headings do it alphabetically through names of subjects in a dictionary catalogue. Subject entries are capable of offering unknown items search through the catalogue. Therefore, the potential usefulness of library material cannot be exploited without subject catalogues. Subject cataloguing and classification are closely related and interlinked.* Therefore, it will be advantageous, if both these tasks are performed by the same person. Subject analysis is the core of both these operations.

Definition

Subject analysis may be defined as the process of determining the specific subject of the document by splitting it into various explicit and implicit thought contents and their mode of presentation. It is the most essential and intellectual part of the process of assigning subject headings. Obviously, it will depend very much on one's wide knowledge of the world of publications and subjects.

---

* For details read "Classification and subject headings" Sears-16, p. xix-xx

Specific subject of a document is defined as the measure of the extension and intension of the subject dealt in the document.

Determination of the specific subject of a document is a diagnostic process. It requires intuitive insights too.

In some documents the specific subject is quite explicit and obvious from the title; in others it lies buried in manifolds. In other cases it is deceptively simple. Whatever be, it always lies and is found within the document – though some outside source may occasionally help in its determination.

Process

To determine the specific subject of the document (for assigning subject headings) some bibliographic parts of the documents are to be scanned in some order beginning with the title of the document.

Title

The first to be examined is the title of the document which is a major source of the subject of the document. AACR–2 defines titles as the chief name of a bibliographic item. Title is the name given to a document which is supposed to indicate its subject contents. It is usually pithy, highly concise even axiomatic statement of the subject contents of a document. In most cases it is densely indicative of the subject of the document, though rarely fully and exactly indicative of the treatment and scope of the subject of the document. As subject indicator a title varies from being plainly simple to highly symbolic or allegorical. Titles may be categorised into three kinds.

Plain Titles

Such titles simply and exactly indicate the subject of the book. Textbooks and reports and journal articles have such titles *e.g.* A Textbook of Boolean algebra; Political thoughts of Plato. Nowadays only a fraction of publications indicate exactly the subject of the document *For example*:

1. Life and times of Shakespeare
2. A textbook of thermodynamics
3. Rudiments of Keynesian economics
4. Vital statistics of Japan
5. A Manual of car repair
6. An Architectural study of the Taj Mahal
7. A Dictionary of library and information science and archives.
8. A Tourist guide to Nepal.

These titles are fully and plainly indicative of the subject of the books. In earlier days the titles used to be very lengthy running even to 20 to 30 words and were fully informative of the subject of the book. *For example:*

1. A classification and subject index for cataloguing and arranging the books and pamphlets of a library (1876).

2. Barracks and Battlefields in India, or the experience of a soldiers of the 10th Foot (North Lincoln) in the Sikh War and Sepoy Mutiny by Rev. Calber Caine 1891.

3. Middle East Crisis. The series of events which preceded the recent crises in the Middle East, and proposal for further western policy by Guy Wint and Peter Calbocoressi. (Penguin 1957).

Titles of unpublished research theses are still lengthy.

Vague titles

Unfortunately this simple and sincere trend under the commercial onslaught has given way to brief, cryptic and vague titles to appeal to a larger circle of readership. Titles are no more determined by authors alone. Publishers, with a view to entice a larger circle of customers insist on a vague, broader, current, catchy titles. These may not be exactly fitting and plain speaking titles. Old innocence is gone – for ever. Now the titles are hardly indicative of the true and exact subject contents of the document. Vague titles indicate broadly the subject and the class of the documents without specifying scope or details. Most of the monographic or journalistic titles belong to this category *e.g.* Shakespeare; India; Man; Earth.

Whether the book is a biography, critical appreciation or an anthology of William Shakespeare is not exactly known from the title. It could even be the title of a play. Similarly, the book entitled "India" is a travelogue in India in 1980's. Numerous other books bear the title "India" with varying subject contents. A book on "Earth" on examination happens to be a book on environment saving. Most of today's books fall in this category. It is now a common experience of the librarians that a title does not at once reveai the real and succinct subject of the document.

Fanciful titles

The third category is of books having catchy or fanciful titles full of literary richness, enticing and intoxicating words. These aesthetically pleasing titles do not easily indicate the subject of the book. Such titles essentially of high literary richness are either symbolic or allegorical having a far fetched and hidden meaning related with the subject contents. Autobiographical and general nonfiction books have usually such titles.

Such titles are either symbolic or allegorical *i.e.* have hidden meaning. Take, *For example*,

The Eagle and the Dragon

It is a book on the foreign relations between USA (Eagle) and China (dragon).

The Future Shock
The Third Wave
Powershift

All these books by Alvin Toffler are on futuristic society. "Silicon idol" is a book on computer and its chips (which are made of silicon). "Asking for troubles" by Amrik Singh is a memoir of a Vice Chancellor of a university in India depicting the awkward situations in which Vice-Chancellors are working. Asian Drama by Gunnar Myrdal is a classic book on Third World poverty. "The Eye of the Serpent" by S. Theodore Bhaskeran is a book on Tamil Cinema. "Dragon in the Land of Snow" is on the invasion of China on Tibet. Curry in the Crown by Shrabani Basu (1999) is a book on places serving Indian dishes in England. Even science and technology books have been seen espousing such titles: "Green Wisdom" by Arthur Galston is a textbook on botany. 'Tiger's milk' is a book on the hard and monotonous routines of a housewife. "The Touch of Midas" edited by Ziauddin Sardar (1997) is volume of conference proceedings on the theme "Science and technology of Islam in on West." The list can be endless. Biographies often have fanciful titles.

On the other hand there may be many superfluous words in the title from the subject viewpoint. *For example*, take the title, "A long and exciting expedition to the Himalayas." Here the "Himalayan Expedition" is the core subject. For the purpose of subject analysis other words carry no weight, howsoever spiritually and emotionally important these may be to the author. Take another example, "Life of Pandit Jawaharlal Nehru: The architect of India's destiny". For subject analysis it is only important to know that it is a biography of Jawaharlal Nehru. There are numerous such examples. In all such cases the title should be stripped off these decorative, or epithetical words which only re-emphasise the stature of the subject. Semantically these are meaningless for subject indexing. It should be borne in mind that we assign subject headings not to the title but to the specific subject of the document. *A title needs augmenting and trimming to adequately and unambiguously indicate the subject of the book.*

So one is never sure whether the title is exactly indicative of the contents of the document. *The Golden Rule is : never rely on the title alone for determining the specific subject of a document : always go beyond the title even if it appears fully true of the subject contents.*

Subtitle

Subtitle is the next place examined for the purpose. It follows the title proper separated by a Colon or any typographical device. Many documents have no subtitles as their titles are fully explanatory of the subject. Subtitle always elucidates or further explains the title proper. It delimits the title proper to make it more precise and specific. Subtitle cannot be independent of the title. Vague and fanciful titles must invariable be followed by a subtitle to indicate more specifically the subject of the document. Here are a few ordinary *examples:*

Jawaharlal Nehru : A biography
History of India : The Mughal Period
Beyond Classification : Book Numbers
Code for classifiers : Principles governing the consistent placing of books in a system of classification.
Irrepressible reformer : Biography of Melvil Dewey

A subtitle is a vital statement for subject analysis.

Other Parts

Even a subtitle may not be hundred per cent indicative of the subject. Too detailed title and subtitle may look inelegant. Therefore, it is imperative for the cataloguer to scan other parts before finalising the subject analysis of the documents. These are : "About the book" blurb, series, preface, the table of contents, index, and scurrying the text from here and there. Author's affiliation and the cited references may also yield some valuable clues to the specific subject of the document.

Published reviews, if any may also be helpful. If all these efforts fail the last resort is to consult a subject expert. In majority of the cases the blurb and the table of contents yield the precise subject of the book in adequate measure.

Context of Analysis

Once the specific subject is known through the above steps, there is further need to determine the field of study in which it falls. We also need to consider the form of the study, limitation of the subject and the viewpoint of the author. Further one has to analyse the subtopics or aspects of the study. Lastly, the media of the document has to be considered. *For example*, a subject say Economics may be treated from the viewpoint of its theory, philosophy, history research; it could be a general introduction to the subject; or it could be the economic conditions of a place or region. It could also be a textbook, dictionary, or a journal of economics; or a mere collection of tabulated data. Not only this, any of the above internal or external arrangement may be published in any physical media, namely a book, a journal, a newspaper clippings, electronic forms such as CD-ROM or a microfiche. Thus, a subject cataloguer has to sort out from the document:

Discipline
Subject : topic : aspect
Specific subject
Form of presentation of the thought
Media of the document.

After this is done, we move onto heart of the job, *i.e.* to assign the analysed subject an appropriate heading from a standard authority list – in our case the Sears List. In fact no subject analysis is absolute. The analysis has to be done in context of Sears. Therefore, the contents, structure and principles of Sears List must be taken in view while doing subject analysis. A subject cataloguer is essentially a match maker. To do this we need to know the organization of the source list : SHs proper, their categories and subdivision and of course the technique to operate it. [This is the very purpose of writing this book and is its essence].

It is a part of subject analysis that viewpoint, or aspect or topical subdivision be distinguished from the subject proper. For this we should at the first instance know the scope of the commonly used subdivisions. Some examples of viewpoints and aspects are given below:

Viewpoints

Economics – Philosophy
Economics – History

Topical aspects

Bible – Astronomy
Bible – Geography
Bible – Inspiration
Bible – Natural history
Bible – Versions
Bible – Parables

Bibliographic forms

Elections – Journal
Elections – Dictionary
Elections – Bibliography
Elections – Maps

The job of assigning subject headings is a practical work which can be divided into two phases :

Subject analysis
Assigning the subject heading.

These two phases can easily be likened to medical diagnosis and prescription. If the problem is correctly and fully diagnosed then the prescription is easy, and many a times a matter of common knowledge. Subject analysis is an intellectual work and needs expertise and experience.

It is the most essential input in the subject access work; and the quality of result will depend upon the quality of this job. It requires wide acquaintance of subjects. In fact the job of subject cataloguing expects practitioners to know something about every subject. In a special library adequate and depth knowledge of the special subject is required . Such knowledge constantly improves with experience though nobody can claim to reach perfection. There is always a scope to learn more. Indeed widely read people have more flair, rather uncanny sights, than others in determining the subject of the document. Growing complexity and variety of subjects and rapidly advancing frontiers of knowledge have, nevertheless, made the task more demanding.

General Procedure for Assigning the Right Heading

Pick up the key words from the title. In case of a unifocal document think of a succinct subject term in natural language : Elections in India is a unifocal subject. Election corruption in India is a subject with an aspect. India is a geographical qualifier.

Whereas, classification in Medical libraries is a complex subject; but flora and fauna of Japan is a compound (here bifocal) subject as per the structure of Sears List. Think of a concise subject heading. Indeed thinking will be facilitated by personal knowledge about subjects and conditioned by the prior knowledge of the organization and scope of the *Sears List*. To make a better acquaintance with the contents and organisation of Sears, it will always be profitable to glance through the Sears off and on, casually and leisurely. Browsing through the list is always rewarding serendipitously and accumulatively. It will result in efficiency and ease of use of the *List* in guessing and then locating the right heading. In fact the structure and contents of the Sears at the back of our mind will guide our subject analysis and help coin better approach terms to locate headings in the *List*.

Scanning the list alphabetically reach the guessed heading. If it is given in bold face then probably you have arrived at the right heading in one go; or to a springboard to jump to the appropriate heading. If you arrive at a light face heading you will be directed to the right heading given against the label "USE". Having arrived at the heading:

1. First look at the class numbers, which may give at least a vague idea of the aptness of the heading.

2. Then read the scope note, if any, which gives further confirmation on the right choice or otherwise of the SH.

3. Then look through the entire entry especially the NTs and RTs. If the entry contain "SA...." note then look through the instructed headings or coin the more specific one as instructed there. "SA..." instruction, if applicable, will lead to more specific, so better, heading. Let us take an example.

A dictionary of Indian flora

Here the key subject word is flora. Dictionary is a bibliographical form included in commonly used subdivisions. India is a geographical delimiter. We look under the term "Flora" – which is a non-preferred heading. We are directed to look under *Botany*, and *Plants*.

Looking under *Botany* the scope note lays down that it is to be used for the "Science of Plants". Looking under the *Plants* we note that it is the appropriate heading. Instruction "May subdivided. Geog" allows it to be geographically subdivided by name of the region/country. Hence our intermediate heading is:

Plants – India

Dictionary is a commonly used subdivision applicable to any subject heading. Hence the final SH is :

Plants – India – Dictiona

Let us take another *example* :

Life of the great English Scientist Isaac Newton

As any person forms a specific entry so it will be entered directly under the personal name. *Life* can be treated as a commonly used subdivision "Biography". For personal names the model SH is Shakespeare, William. On this analogy we get

Newton, Isaac, 1642-1727 – Biography.

Here the words great even English scientist are redundant. This heading can also be arrived at when we look through its specific subject *i.e.* scientist

Scientists : 509.2; 920

SA types of scientists and names of individual scientists to be added as needed.

Hence, we can add the name of Isaac Newton in the form prescribed by Sears

There may be cases that even after very correctly analysing the subject of the book and picking up key words from the title, subtitle, or from the blurb the matching with the Sears headings yields no result. There may seem no relevant SH for the purpose.

It may happen on many accounts, *e.g.*, the subject may be a new one for which yet no term has yet been settled and included in the Sears.

Guidance for tackling such cases has been given in the "Principles" under the section "New Subjects" (pp. xxxvi). But more importantly the Sears at times uses some terms other than anticipated by the cataloguers. *For example*

Pay of clerical staff

Pay is a common Indian term for salary but looking under it one finds no such term. Then we look under any of the other synonymous terms *i.e.* Salary, Wages, Looking under *Salary* we draw a blank, but its plural salaries is given in light face

Salaries
Use Wages

So we look under *wages* which is the right heading. It is a bifocal book in context of Sears. Under *Wages* there is no instruction to link it with the kind of wage earner. So we look under clerical staff and are directed to use the SH *Office workers*. Hence the two SHs are :

Wages; Office workers

Use a broader heading if no suitable heading is found. Scan the NTs and RTs of the broader heading and also follow the "SA" (See also) instructions. May be further scanning leads you to a better heading. If not content with the broader heading then use two or more headings which may describe the subject.

In fact, this is too facile a view of the process of assigning subject headings to a document. In reality even an experienced subject cataloguer may encounter many unanticipated and baffling difficulties. Sometimes the subject of the document may be too deep and complex, and highly composite with many aspects and facets. Many a time it may be too vague. Another could be a patently new subject not finding even a remote mention in the subject analysis tools. And there is a perennial problem of subjects specifically belongings to a local and unique culture which cannot be dealt with an out and out American system like Sears List or the Dewey Decimal Classification. *For example*, child marriage is a hot topic at the moment in India, but in Sears there is no entry for this topic. Obviously there is no logarithm to mechanically do the subject analysis and assign subject headings to a document. S R Ranganathan's eight steps, though meant for practical classification, may be profitably adapted for subject headings work. These may be modified as follows.*

* S R Ranganathan, *Colon Classification*, 6th ed. Bombay : Asia, 1969. Pp. 1.7-1.8.

Step 0 : Raw title, as it appears on the title page

(a) Invincible Eliot

(b) A long and exciting expedition to the Himalayas

Step 1: Full title . Title made expressive by the cataloguer by addition of implied words :

(a) Invincible (TS) Eliot 1885-1965 – the American poet: A critical study of his life.

(b) A long and exciting expedition to the Himalayan (region) : a travelogue : Geography)

Step 2: Kernel title. Full title minus all the auxiliary or apparatus words with composite terms broken into fundamental terms.

(a) T S Eliot, 1888-1965. American poet. Biography

(b) Expedition. Travelogue. Himalayan region. Geography

Step 3 : Analysed title. Kernel title is analysed in terms of discipline, subject, its aspects, common subdivisions and media of the document.

T S Eliot, 1888-1965. Life (Common subdivision)
Himalayan region. Geography. Travel. Common subdivision

Step. 4 : Transformed title. Here the analysed title is rearranged in the General to specific order followed by topical, chronological, and form subdivisions.

Eliot, T. S., 1888-1965. Life
Himalayan region. Travelogue

Step 5 : Title in standard terms and punctuations

In context of subjects headings work this is the last and final step to use the standard terms used in the authority list and replace the terms in our title with standard terminology of the authority List. (Here Sears):

Eliot, T.S., 1888-1965- Biography
Himalayas - Travels

These are standard subject headings.

In the subject headings work Ranganathan's remaining steps belonging to notation and retranslation (for verification) are redundant.

In the beginning this step by step procedure appears, dead slow, dull and even circumlocutious process. But it is of many advantages to the learner; an experienced cataloguer may take many steps mentally. Nevertheless, some practice in these steppy procedure makes you an adept subject cataloguer and Sears operator.

Still there may be difficulties in the subject headings work, especially in case of subjects whose headings are not listed especially in the *Sears List.* In such cases the cataloguers should keep in mind the list of "Headings to be added by the cataloguer" (p. xxxvii). The list is long, varied and veiled. The categories in this list should be on one's fingertips for efficiency. This is in addition to the key headings which provide patterns for coining subject headings

Yet another formidable and challenging task may be faced in case of new subjects for terms which have not been standardized in current literature, so are far from being listed. Guidance in such situations has been given in the Sears-16 in the "Principles" under the section "New subjects" at page xxxvi.

Multifocal Documents

Monographs and textbooks usually deal with a single topic, *e.g.* A textbook of Astronomy: History of Medieval Europe; Principles of library Classification. Numerous documents are multifocal and composite in nature dealing with many topics. *For example,* A handbook of libraries information centres and archives; A textbook of library classification and cataloguing.

Some subjects, though not really composite are multifocal and are not covered by one single topic : Corrupt practices in elections for the Parliament. Surface Transportation of Agriculture products; Darwin and the Social Sciences; Psychology for doctors and nurses; Computer application in libraries are some of the obvious titles in this category. Titles could be highly multifocal especially in case of doctoral and other research reports, *e.g.* "School drop out rates among the lower middle class urban Muslim children of South India'.

Most of the subjects by nature and in implied way make significant reference to other subjects while dealing with one definite subject. Some subjects intrinsically burrow into other related subjects. *For example,* the politics of Jawaharlal Nehru is also a chapter of Indian history; A book on "housing for the poor" deals with Housing as well as social poverty. Life of Mother Teresa (1910- 1997) is also intimately linked with the social work of Christian missionaries. History of British India is also a chapter of British colonialism. A history of Sikhs is also history of Punjab. A book on history of science may have a detailed chapter on history of mathematics. It is known as analytical subject cataloguing. In fact to discover and highlight such relations is the essence of intelligent library work; and makes the subject analysis work a truly intellectual task.

It is no problem to deal with such composite and multifocal subjects. It simply means that such documents should be assigned more than one subject heading. Practically, there is no problem or hitch in assigning any number of subject headings to a document as may be required to comprehensively cover the subject(s) of the document. Since we assign subject headings not to the documents but to their surrogates, therefore, for a document as many surrogates may be created as may be desired.

Number of subject headings to be assigned to a

document depends upon many factors.

The factor which determine the number of subject headings are: Nature of the document; scarcity of reading material on a given subject; manpower availability; level of users; and of course on the form of the library catalogue whether in card or book on computerised form. Number of added entries in card catalogue, even in book form catalogue is restrained to save the catalogues from getting bulky. There is no such problem in OPACs. In computerised catalogue we prepare only one entry which has many access points. Upto three subject headings are considered normal. In a research and industrial library the number of subject headings could be up to ten or more. The problem has been dealt in the "Principles" under the section "Classification and Subject Headings" (p. xix).

Therefore, every library has to formulate an internal policy regarding the number of surrogates to be prepared of a document, and consequently, the number of subject headings to be assigned.

Use of more than one Heading

Scholastically speaking no single subject heading can exhaustively cover all the subjects treated in a document. E. J. Coates rightly says: "This would not be possible without causing the heading for each document to rival the document itself in elaboration and complexity and without raising the cost of cataloguing and catalogue consultation to a prohibitively high level."* Hence to cover the subject contents fairly exhaustively even for a monograph a research library may assign more than one heading; and indeed a multifocal book will need many more subject headings.

Unlike call numbers subject headings are not applied on the document themselves but on their surrogates. For a document many surrogates can be created and

---

* E. J. Coates, *Subject Catalogues*. London : Library Association Publishing, 1988, p. 15.

different surrogates may be given different subject headings. Thus, there is no physical constraint on the number of headings to be given on a document. In fact, a subject catalogue in addition to other functions make up one deficiency of call number which assign a document to one and only one place on the shelf. Subject headings can be placed at different places simultaneously. Subject catalogue is a retrieval device, not a location tool.

How many Subject Headings

It is an unsolved question which depends upon many factors such as nature and complexity of the document; level of users; strength of the reading material in that area, and above all an arbitrary policy of the library restricting them to a predetermined number. Recall ratio of a search will depend upon the number of subject headings given to a document. Since no subject catalogue can give a full statement of the subjects available in a library, so recall ratio is always less than one. In a research library the users want a comprehensive search on a given topic. It will be appropriate to give as many SHs as possible. It may depend upon the type of material: research reports, newspaper clippings, journal articles. Academic theses may require more subject headings per unit document. A composite book dealing with many topics may require as many SHs as the number of chapters. Strength of library material on a topic in a particular library determines the number; lesser the number of documents in a library more the subject headings required by way of analytical entries to bring to surface the material lying buried in a chapter or even section of a document. More SHs means providing more subject access points. This will lead to enhanced *recall ratio.* Some libraries have predetermined policy to restrict the number of headings whatever be the document or its subject contents. Magic number is three – though research libraries may use five or more; and a school/small public library may use only one.

Summary

Subject analysis forms the essential ground work for subject headings work. It may be defined as formulating the subject and its subtopics and aspects and the media of the document. Subject of the document may be determined mostly from the title, subtitle, book blurb, table of contents and the subject index. Bookreviews and experts are the last resort. Titles are not only vague and inadequate, but sometimes look deceptively simple. Fanciful titles, which are allegorical or symbolic, are gaining ground under the onslaught of marketing and commercialism. Therefore, a golden rule is not to go by the title alone for subject analysis. Subject analysis has to be done in context of the structure and contents of the Sears List. It requires wide knowledge of subjects and looks mostly a matter of flair. It improves with experience. S.R. Ranganathan's Eight Steps for practical classification may be adapted for subject headings work. Documents usually enshrine multifocal, and complex subjects explicitly or implicitly. It is an intellectual work of high order to bring to surface and highlight the hidden topics in a document and to correlate them with the main subject. Such documents obviously require more than one subject heading. There is no problem in assigning more than one subject heading to a document as the situation may demand. Number of subject headings may be restricted by a policy which in turn depends upon factors like strength of collection in a given subject, levels of users, and an arbitrary restriction on the number of subject headings. In a small public library it could be one, in a special or research library it could be as many as ten. Average number of subject headings in an academic or a large public library may be three.

Exercise

1. Define subject analysis
2. Name the sources, in order, to be scanned for determining the subject of a document.

3. State the categories of titles appearing in print.

4. Name Ranganathan's steps adapted to subject headings work.

5. How the multifocal documents are tackled for subject indexing work?

6

KEY HEADINGS

Key headings are model headings which provide a clear and readymade pattern to coin analogous subject headings. Though key headings are implicitly included in the categories of omitted headings but these have also been listed separately because of their literary warrant and many unique specific or topical subdivisions. These key headings as given on page xl (Sear 16) are for: Presidents/Prime Ministers, Prolific authors, Peoples, Places, Languages, and Literature, and wars. The key headings for these categories are:

Author	:	Shakespeare, William, 1564-1616
Presidents	:	Presidents – United States
Places		
Country	:	United States
State/Province	:	Ohio
City	:	Chicago (Ill)
Language	:	English language
Wars and battles	:	World War, 1939-1945
Peoples	:	Indians of North America

In the Sears-14 and earlier Kennedy, John F had also been used as a key heading for persons of noted families. Now it has been omitted. Subdivisions specific to these headings have been listed under each, and apply to all the headings to be coined on that pattern. Subdivisions may also be adopted in the new headings to be coined on the pattern of kev headings.

To use these key headings, first of all a cataloguer has to keep in mind the category of these headings. So, for a subject of any of these categories we have to look under the corresponding key heading. Let us say, our title is Constitutional History of India.

Since it pertains to a country, so we will look under the key heading for a country, *viz.*, United States. Scanning the various subdivisions of the heading United States we hit at *United States –Constitutional history*: Here we will substitute India for the United States and get the heading.

India – Constitutional history

Similarly we can have SHs like Sri Lanka-Constitutional history.

Trinidad and Tobago – Constitutional history
Bosnia-Herzegovina-Constitutional history

Let us take another example,

Rajya Sabha

Rajya Sabha is the upper house of the Indian Parliament. Since it pertains to a country. So we will again look under United States. The corresponding heading now is:

United States. Congress. Senate. We will replace the above three constitutional terms by the appropriate Indian terms to form *India. Parliament. Rajya Sabha* (It may be reminded that the headings are in the form prescribed by AACR-2(1978).

Quit India movement, 1942

This is a topic pertaining to history of India. We look under United States-History to coin the following headings.

History of British rule in India
India–History–1757-1947, British rule
India's Foreign Policy towards Pakistan: A bibliography

we will use the pattern:

United States–Foreign relations

Thus, the SH is

Indian – Foreign relations – Pakistan – Bibliography
A catalogue of the Government Publications of China.
Government Publications – China – Bibliography

Let us take another subject

Recruitment procedure in the Indian Army. Again it pertains to a country. Looking under the United States we locate the corresponding heading as:

United States. Army–Recruitment, enlisting, etc. Accordingly our heading will be.

India. Army – Recruitment, enlisting, etc.

Take another book

Gazetteer of Tamil Nadu

Tamil Nadu is an Indian State, so will look under the key state *i.e.* Ohio. There the appropriate heading is

Ohio–Gazetteers

Take another example

Geography of Jammu and Kashmir

Under Ohio there is no subdivision as geography. So we look under the heading geography. Under this heading apart from other instructions, it is informed that "materials limited" to a particular place are entered under the name of the place with the subdivisions geography". Hence our subject heading will be.

Jammu and Kashmir–Geography

On this analogy we may have SHs:

India–Geography
South Asia–Geography
Nilgiri Hills–Geography
Ganga River–Geography
Indian Ocean–Geography

Let us take another *example*:

Dictionary of Folk songs of Hawaii.

Since it pertains to a state, so we look under Ohio, and the appropriate subdivisions. We are directed to look under folk songs where there is an instruction to divide it geographically. Hence our SH is.

Folk songs–Hawaii–Dictionary

Take another *example*,

A bibliography on the sources of history of Bavaria

Bavaria–History–Sources–Bibliography

The subdivision history, if needed, could further be subdivided chronologically:

A bibliography on the sources of history of Bavaria from 1815 to 1866.

Bavaria–History–1815-1866–Sources–Bibliography.

Similarly,

Social life in New South Wales

Looking under Ohio, the appropriate heading is

Ohio –Social life and customs

So our heading is

New South Wales–Social life and customs

Let us take an example pertaining to a city.

Town planning in Karachi

For this we look under Chicago to find the entry: Chicago (Ill)–City planning

Since the heading is given in light face, so it cannot be used as heading. We are instead directed to

City planning – Chicago (Ill)

Our corresponding heading thus, will be:

City planning – Karachi

Let us take another heading

Directory of industries in Manchester

Since it pertains to a city so we look under Chicago (Ill) to find an entry

Chicago (Ill)–Industries

It is in light type face and we are directed to use:

Industries–Chicago (Ill.)

So our required heading will be

Industries–Manchester – Directories

Some other heading pertaining to a city could be

Mumbai–Telephone directories

Chennai–Biography

Kathmandu–Guide books
(for tourist guides to Kathmandu, Nepal)

Amritsar–Statistics
(for general statistics of Amritsar)

History of New York City

New York (N.Y.)–History

Population statistics of Paris city

Paris–Population–Statistics

Statistics here is a common subdivision.

Directory of foreigners in Cape Town

Cape Town–Foreign population–Directory

Key Heading for People

For people the key heading is

Indians of North America

Let us take the heading

Dances of Nagas

Naga–Dances

Folklore of Khasis of Assam

Khasis of Assam–Folklore

Ceremonies of Rajputs of Punjab

Rajputs of Punjab–Rites and ceremonies

Ceremonies of Rajputs of Rajasthan

Rajputs of Rajasthan–Rites and ceremonies

Costumes of Eskimos

Eskimos–Costume

Key Heading for Persons

There are two types of key headings for two different categories of persons. The first is

Heads of State: Presidents – United States.

This heading is also applicable to Prime Ministers, Rulers, and other variously named heads of states such as Kings, Chancellor, Shahs, and the like. Here the U.S. may be substituted by the appropriate country and subdivisions 'President' may be substituted by the appropriate local terms for the executive power.

Take, for example Election of the Chancellor of Germany.

We look under President – United States and have the following appropriate heading.

Presidents–United States–Election

So our corresponding heading will be : *Chancellors–Germany–Election.*

Financial cost of security cover given to the Prime Minister of India:

Prime Minister–India–Protection–Cost.

Here Security corresponds to protection, as given under the key headings and 'cost' is a commonly used subdivisions.

Biographies of kings of Nepal

Kings–Nepal–Biography

Intellectual lives of kings and queens of England.

Monarchs–England–Intellectual life

Collected speeches of Nawab of Hyderabad

Nawabs–Hyderabad–Messages

Powers of Prime Minister of India

Executive power–India

The second category is of prolific authors represented by *Shakespeare, William, 1564–1616*

Take some examples of literary authors.

Encyclopaedia of Robert Browning

Browning, Robert, 1812–1890 – Dictionaries

A study in the styles of Prem Chand

Prem Chand, 1880–1940–Technique

A Critical interpretation of the works of Amrita Pritam

Amrita Pritam, 1917 – Criticism

Characters of G B Shaw's plays

Shaw, George Bernard, 1860-1956 – Characters

A Critical study of the works of Rabindra Nath Tagore.

Tagore, Rabindra Nath, 1861-1941 – Criticism

Keats understanding of Greek mythology.

Keats, John, 1795-1821–Knowledge – Greek mythology.

Literary technique of Prem Chand

Prem Chand – 1880-1940 – Technique

Quotations from Alexander Pope the great neo–classical poet.

Pope, Alexander, 1688–1744– Quotations

Key Heading for Wars and Battles

Key headings for war and battles is

World War 1939-1945

On this analogy SHs for any war or battle may be coined, *e.g.*

Causes of the Gulf War, 1991

Gulf War, 1991– Causes

As per instructions World War, 1914-1918 is to be divided, if needed, like, World War, 1939-1945. So we may have headings like

World War, 1914-1918–Refugees

World War, 1914-1918–Causes

World War, 1914-1918–Battlefields

World War, 1914-1918–Food supply – Administration

In the later case 'Administration' is a commonly used subdivision.

Battlefields of the war between India and Pakistan in 1965.

Indo-Pak War, 1965 – Battlefields.

Economic consequences of the Battles of Plassey.

Plassey Battle, 1742 – Economic aspects

Indo-Pak War of 1971 in Pictures

Indo-Pak War, 1971 – Pictorial works.

On this analogy subject headings for any war or battle and their varied aspects may be easily coined.

Key heading for places, and languages, and literature have been treated separately.

Summary

Key heading provide a pattern for other heading in that class. On the analogy of that model subject headings for corresponding subject heading may be coined simply by replacing the lead component by the specific headings. These are listed in the beginning on page xl (Sears -16). These headings as full entries and their specific subdivisions are listed in the main list at their alphabetical place.

These are for

Person	:	Presidents - United States Shakespeare, William, 1564-1616
Places:		
Country	:	United States
State	:	Ohio
City	:	Chicago (Ill)
Languages	:	English language
Literature	:	English literature
People	:	Indians of North America
Wars	:	World War 1939-1945

Exercise

Find the subject heading for

1. Chronology of Indian Prime Ministers
2. A bibliography on the art of George Bernard Shaw (1856-1950)
3. Folklore of Naga people
4. History of India from 1857-1957
5. Government of People's Republic of China
6. Population Atlas of Orissa
7. Telephone directory of Calcutta
8. Causes of the Third Battle of Panipat
9. World politics since 1998
10. Causes of the Crimean war

7

CATEGORIES OF HEADINGS OMITTED

> "It is only by being flexible and expandable that Sears has been able over the years to fill the needs of various kinds of libraries".
>
> (Preface, Sears-16, p. x)

The principle of specific and direct entry makes it practically impossible for any general list of subject headings to list all possible subject headings to be used in a catalogue.

Even a specialised list such as MeSH cannot do it. "No list can possibly provide a heading for every idea, object, process or relationship. What the *Sears* hopes to offer is a basic list that incorporates pattern and example that will guide the cataloguer in adding new headings". Sears-16, p. ix.

Accordingly numerous other headings can be derived from the Sears, though not explicitly listed. A subject with a common name, *e.g.* University, Automobile, Monument, Presidents, can be listed, but subjects like Robert Gordon University, Ronald Regan, or Presidents–India, Rolls Royce, The Taj Mahal cannot be listed in any general system of subject headings for obvious reasons–they are too numerous and always keep emerging in hoards. Subjects with proper or specific names though quite fit to form SHs are not listed in the Sears. Therefore, the Sears list is not only a repertoire of subject headings but also provides patterns and mechanism to coin subject headings for omitted headings. Reasons and advantages of providing patterns and instructions in coining SHs are:

(a) No forehand list can be made of all the specific or proper names of entities or concepts. New subjects and names keep constantly emerging in large numbers.

(b) Thoroughness in coverage is ensured.

(c) Saves enormous space in the list and immunes it from getting unwieldy or bulky.

(d) Provides autonomy to the cataloguers; keeps the subject work going even in the face of new and unprovided subjects.

(e) Makes the subject heading work more creative, imaginative and intellectually stimulating.

Broadly speaking the headings which may be coined by the cataloguers may be divided into two categories:

1. Categories for which key headings have been provided on the pattern of these key headings for People, Presidents, Prolific authors, Countries, Provinces, Cities, Languages, Literatures, and Wars can be formulated by substitution of the desired word/term in the key headings listed on page xl of Sears-16.

2. The second category is of totally omitted headings; only their classes are listed. Headings for individual members by specific names have to be coined. In fact such names are headings in themselves. Subject having specific name belonging to any class of objects, by the rule of specific entry, can become a subject heading.

The list of categories of classes omitted in Sears has been given in the section "Headings to be Added by the Cataloguer" (p. xxxix, Sears-16). This list has been divided into: (a) Proper names, (b) Common names.

For example:

Plato
Jawaharlal Nehru, 1889-1964

Elizabeth Taylor
Presidency College, Calcutta
Indian Library Association
Bhartiya Janata Party
African National Congress
All India Radio
Apollo Circus
Indian Airlines
Sahara India (Airlines)
World Book Fair
Delhi Cloth Mill
Empire State Building
Eifel Tower
India
Bangalore
Karnataka
United Nations Organisation
Victoria Falls
Grand Canyon
The Mississippi River
The Himalayan Mountains
The Mount Everest
Atlantic Ocean
Gobi Desert
The Taj Mahal
Fortran
C Language
Rolls Royce

These are only a few names, which can also work as SHs, and may be subdivided further as per rules, if needed.

Names of Associations, Societies, Clubs, Conferences, Symposia, Meets, Fairs, Exhibitions form their SHs as such:

Royal Chemical Society–History
University of Texas at Austin–Awards
Association of Indian Universities
International Federation of Library

Associations and Institutions (IFLA)
Lions Club–Chronology
Federation of Indian Publishers
Olympic Games–History
Frankfurt Book Fair–Statistics

All the above names can form SHs. Similarly, names of institutions, educational institutions, hospitals, hotels, business, houses, industrial units, newspapers, ships, are fit to become SHs:

British Broadcasting Corporation
Don Bosco School (Shillong)
New York Tribune
The Times
Christian Medical College and Hospital (Ludhiana)
The Missionaries of Charity
Maruti Udyog Limited
Hindustan Lever Limited
General Electric Company
H.W. Wilson Company
Bell Laboratories
Microsoft, Inc.

Though not explicitly mentioned, the names of language families are fit to be subject headings and may be divided by commonly used subdivisions, if needed.

Indo-Aryan languages–Alphabets
Dravdian languages–History
Celtic languages–Grammar

B. Common names from such categories as:

1.	Animals	:	Pandas, Kangaroos, Dogs, Alsatian, Tigers, Lions, Cattle
2.	Birds	:	Parrots, Crows, Swallows, Peacocks, Ostriches, Pigeons, Penguins
3.	Fishes	:	Trot, Salmon
4.	Flowers	:	Marigold, Tulip, Roses

5.	Foods	:	Milk, Yoghurt, Bread, Chocolate, Fruit, Honey, Vegetables, Butter
6.	Beverages	:	Alcoholic Beverages, Coca Cola, Coffee, Tea, Liquors
7.	Fruits	:	Apples, Mangoes, Berries, Citrus, Fruits
8.	Vegetables	:	Gourds, Pumpkins, Green Peas, Brinjals, Carrots, Potatoes
9.	Cereals and Grams	:	Kidney Beans, Grams
10.	FoodGrains	:	Wheat, Maize, Rice
11.	Trees	:	Pine, Oak, Mango, Cedar, Beech, Birch, Chestnut, Tropical Trees, Teak, Sandalwood.
12.	Nuts	:	Pecans, Almonds, Brazil Nuts,Hazel Nuts, Chestnuts, Peanuts, Cashewnuts, Walnuts
13.	Games	:	Cricket, Football, Tennis, Polo, Ice Hockey, Chess, Volleyball, Rugby
14.	Sports	:	Cycling, Horse racing, Discus throw, Tug of war, Swimming, Long Jump
15.	Musical Instruments	:	Guitar, Harmonium, Violin, Sitar, Veena, Drums, Clarinet.
16.	Tools	:	Saws, Pliers, Machine tools
17.	Dances	:	Rock n' roll, Bharat Natayam, Odissi, Bhangra, Bamboo dance.
18.	National musics	:	Jazz music, American music,Indian music
19.	Names of artefacts	:	Last supper, Monalisa, Rock garden.
20.	Monuments and buildings	:	Taj Mahal, Pyramids, Great Wall of China, Empire State Building, Red Fort, London Bridge, Statue of Liberty.
21.	Names of Diseases	:	Malaria, Cancer, Aids, Small pox, Myopia, Amnesia

22.	Names of organs and regions of body :	Heart, liver,lungs, legs, chest, fingers, hair, face, eyes
23.	Names of chemicals and minerals :	Sulphuric acid, Calcium carbonate, DDT, DNA, Sulphates, Chlorides, Topaz, Diamonds, Rubies, Silicon
24.	Chemical elements :	Oxygen, Carbon, Copper, Silver, Uranium, Radium, Curium, Mercury Chlorine
25.	Place names :	Europe, Euro Asia, Asia, South Asia, South Africa, India, West Bengal, Calcutta
26.	Political, geographical or cultural groups of countries :	Scandinavian countries, Aberian Peninsula, Arabian countries, G-8, European Union, SAARC countries Baltic states, West Indies,
27.	Geographical features such as mountains, hills, valleys, lakes, rivers, oceans, seas, Islands, Archipelagoes, capes river mouths,falls :	Atlantic ocean, North Sea, Baltic Sea, Dead Sea, The Ganga (River) Gobi desert, Falkland Island, English Channel, Mouth of Ganga, Victoria Falls
28.	Names of nationalities, ethnic and racial groups :	South Asians, Nepalis, Japanese, Finns, Dutchs, Swedes, Afghans, Mongols, Aryans, Dravadians, Khasis, Arabs, Hindus, Jews, Blacks, Roman Catholics, Lapps, Eskimos, Nagas, Maories
29.	National languages and literatures :	Commonwealth literature, Canadian literature, Indian literature in English, French literature, Dravidian literature

30.	Names of wars and Battles	:	World War II, War of Roses, Crimean War, Battle of Panipat I, Battle of Plassey, Battle of the Ardennes
31.	Names of Famous Agreement treaties and trials	:	Tashkent treaty, Shimla Agreement; Nuremberg Trials, Earth Summit

The list is not exhaustive, In fact, any proper or common name is a SH. When such a self coined subject heading is created it should be immediately entered alongwith cross references in the library's copy of the Sears List. Such a checked in page has been given as sample in Sears at page xiv. It works as an authority list.

Let us say we are to find a subject heading for a book on Mangoes fruit. In the Sears there is no entry under Mango/ Mangoes. Then we look under its class, *viz.* fruit.

Fruit 634; 641.3

SA types of fruit, *e.g.* Berries; citrus fruits; etc. and names of fruit, *e.g.* apple to be added as needed in the singular form for tree fruit.

It is clear that we can add the heading "Mango" of our own and record it in the Sears. The full entry will thus be:

Mango

SA Species of mangoes *e.g. Langra, Dusheri, Alphanso*

BT Fruit

At about 500 places in the Sears, "SA" instructions have been added permitting cataloguers to coin headings of greater specificity. Let us take another example, Capsicum. It is a vegetable and there exists no entry under it. Then we look under its class, *viz.*

Vegetables 635; 641.3

SA types of vegetables to be added as needed. As another clue, under the NT term *Potatoes* has been given. Similarly we can coin the heading *Capsicums* and add it in the list. (see appendix)

Let us take another example

Atlas of Pine trees in India

There is no entry under Pine in the Sears. We look under its class Trees, where instructions exist to subdivide the SH *Trees* geographically. Then under the label we are permitted to add, whenever needed, names of trees such as Oak (Name are to be added in singular form). *More importantly, we also assume that since its class "Trees" is subdivisible geographically so individual trees* can also be subdivided *geographically*. So our heading will be:

Pine – India – Atlas

Atlas is a commonly used subdivisions. Let us take another such example.

Training for *Ice fishing* in Finland

There is no entry under *Ice – fishing*. Looking under its broader class *i.e.* Fishing we have

Fishing (May subdiv. Geog) 799.1 use for material on fishing as a sport.......

UF Angling

SA types of fishing to be added as needed.

So we choose our heading as Ice-fishing. Since Fishing is subdivisible geographically, so we form the heading

Icefishing – Finland

Further *Training* is a commonly used subdivision, so our final heading is

Icefishing – Finland – Training

Some more examples

History of Indian Library Association, 1933-1983

It is an association with a specific name, so will form the heading by itself. History is a common subdivision. Thus, the SH is :

Indian Library Association – History – 1933-1983

The other way is to look under its class *i.e.* Associations.

Associations (May subdiv. Geog.) *060*; 30203;366

SA –; and names of specific associations to be added as needed.

Hence, we can form the SH *Indian Mathematical Association* and subdivide it further, if needed. But a title such as Directory of mathematical associations will get the heading.

Mathematics–Societies–Directories

Let us take another example

Pandit Ravi Shankar's *My Life and My Music* will get the SH.

Shankar, Ravi, 1920 – Biography

This is the most specific heading for the book. Inevitably it contains sufficient description of the Indian music of which he is a great exponent then we can have additional heading for the music. For this we look under the SH:

Music	*780*
UF	Classical music
SA	Music of particular countries, *e.g.* American music; types of music *e.g. Vocal music*

On this pattern we can have subject headings

Indian music, *instrumental music* and also *Sitar music*

Geography of Shivalik Hills

There is no entry under *Hills*; we look under the related term *Mountains*

Mountains (May subdiv. geo.) 551.4

SA Names of mountain ranges and of individual mountains to be added as needed

On this instruction we can coin the SH *Shivalik Hills* or *Western Ghats*. Again under the SH Geography we have

Geography 910

... Metarial limited to a particular place are entered under the name of the place with the subdivision Geography.

It means *Geography* is also a subdivision for geographical place names. Hence our complete SH is :

Shivalik Hills – Geography

As another example

Physical Chemistry of Calcium

It is a compound heading. The SH *Physical Chemistry* has been listed. Hence, it will be used as a heading. But there is no entry under calcium.

Then we look under chemical elements

Chemical elements 546

SA Names of chemical elements to be added as needed

Hence, as said earlier, names of all chemical elements can be used as SHs. Thus, our other SH will be *Calcium.* Hence, the two SHs of this composite subject will be:

Physical Chemistry

Calcium

So the instruction SA [see also].......... names/ types............ "to be added as needed" is our sure guide for coining headings for which only classes have been given. Coining of such headings should be subject to the principles of Sears, which to repeat, are : specific, direct and consistently uniform headings; currency is another important principle. On this basis numerous SHs can be coined for use whenever and wherever warranted. Number of headings to be thus coined is unlimited.

Brand Names of Commercial Products

Brand names of commercial products and services are also used as SHs. For all these are the SHs

Ford motors
Maruti - Suzuki Automobile
Philvision TV
Rolls Royce – Design and construction
Bofors guns
Singer sewing machine
BMW Motorcycle
IBM computers
Coca Cola

In the Sears illustrated instructions, for coining specific headings of above categories, have been included in that class or form. *For example*, for forming SH for Rolls Royce one should look under its class *Cars* or *Motor cars* – whatever term the Sears uses. From both these headings we are directed to *Automobiles* (p. 70).

Automobiles 338.3; 629.222

UF Cars (Automobiles)
Motor Cars

SA Names of specific makes and models *e.g. Ford Automobiles* to be added as needed.

Hence, we will use Rolls Royce automobile as a heading and also add it in the cataloguer's copy of the Sears. It may be further subdivided by any of the commonly used subdivision or the subdivisions of the class heading:

Ford automobile – Design and construction
Rolls Royce automobile – Brakes
Suzuki automobile – Fuel consumption
Cheverlet automobile – Museum

Names of religious denominations, sects, churches, are SHs

Sikhs – History
Church of England – Biography
Westminster Abbey – Building

Name of Projects, missions, are also from SHs.

Tennese Valley Project
Sardar Sarovar Dam Project – Environmental aspects.

In brief any proper/specific name of any entity can form a SH:

Rosetta Stone
Dead Sea Scrolls
Magna Carta
Shalimar gardens
The Empire State Building
Eifel Tower
Tinneman Square
Nelson Square
Piccadelly Circus
The Palace on Wheel (Train)
Air India
HMS Vikrant

Summary

No subject heading list, whether general or special, can list all possible subject headings. Accordingly, Sears lists some of the SHs (rather classes of headings) and provides mechanism and models for coining the kinds and species belonging to that class. Number of SHs to be coined on the basis of a model or instructions far exceeds the number of headings listed in the Sears. One category of unlisted SHs belonging to the family of key headings is given on page xi of the Sears-16. Seven key headings are for Presidents/Prime Ministers, Prolific authors (Shakespeare) Peoples (Indians of North America), Geopolitical division (Countries, States/ Provinces, cities/towns). Languages and literature (English is the key heading) and for Wars the key heading is World War, 1939-1943. *For example*, subject heading for Sanskrit Grammar, though not given in the list, is formulated on the model of English language – Grammar. So in our case by substituting Sanskrit for English we get the SH *Sanskrit language – Grammar.* Similarly many headings can be formulated for any of the topics falling in the purview of these seven key headings which provide clear and explicit pattern.

Another category of subject headings which can be formulated but are not listed in the Sears are of names (both common and proper) of entities. (This category also impliedly assimilates key headings). A specific name (both taxanomic and given) be it of a person, organisation, system, living or nonliving entity, product, object, (both natural and artificial) body organ and what not, are fit to form subject headings of their own. Such subjects have not been listed in the Sears, but their categories have been listed on page xxxix of Sears-16. Some names of such classes (with example of their kinds or species given in parenthesis) are as follows: Names of persons (Robert Frost), families (Huxleys) Geographical and geographical entities and regions (West Asia, India, Kerala, Bangalore, Antarctica, Gobi desert, Victoria falls, Indian Ocean, Persian Gulf, Cape Comarin, Himalayas, Mount Everest, The Thames). National, racial or ethnic groups (Germans, German Jews, Lapps, Mongols, Maories, South Asians), Wars (World War I), Events (Nuremburg trials; Watergate scandal), Summits and treaties [Tashkent agreement (1966), Earth Summit (Rio de Janeiro). Social, technological and literary movements (Women Lib; Industrial Revolution; Green Revolution (India); Renaissance; Romantic movement. Corporate bodies (Government of Pakistan; Japan Library Association; Apollo Hospital (Chennai); Jawaharlal Nehru University; Indian National Congress; International Conference on Classification Studies and Research. National literature (Scandinavian literature;

French Literature). In addition common names and their specific-species such as cats (Siamese cats), birds (Parrots, Pigeon, Ostriches), Animals (Lions, Tigers, Deer), cattle (Cows) Fruits (Apple), Vegetables (Brinjal), Flowers (Marigold), Trees (Oak), Nuts (Almonds), Sports, Games, Athletics (Hockey, Cycling, Swimming, Chess, Boxing, Discus throw), Body organs (Head, nose liver, heart, hair), Diseases (Malaria, Cancer, Aids) Minerals and chemicals (Oxygen, Gold, Calcium carbonate, DDT, DNA, Silicon, Marble) Brand names (BMW motor cycle, Philvision TV, Sony VCR). The list is not exhaustive. These names may be used as such as subject headings, and may be further divided, if needed. In case of doubt look under the class. *For example* to assign SH to Rolls Royce, we look under its class *Automobiles*. There under SA label there is an instruction to add names of models and makes as SHs. There is given an example of Ford automobiles. On this analogy we coin the SH *Rolls Royce automobiles*. Similarly by looking under vegetables, we can coin SHs such as Potatoes, Capsicum, Gourd, Cabbage, etc. Looking under mountain we coin headings for Himalayas or Url mountains, or Mount Viso. There are about 500 SA [see also] instructions. Such omissions in Sears make the schedule slim without loss of information or effectiveness. Further provision of such implied headings makes the SH work intellectually stimulating and creative. Indeed it provides autonomy to cataloguers and keeps the work going in face of new subjects.

Exercise

1. What is the importance of those SHs, which though have not been listed in the Sears, yet can be added by a cataloguer.

2. Find SHs for

   (a) Cycling as a hobby

   (b) Reading as a hobby

(c) Testing of atomic bomb

(d) Encyclopaedic dictionary of sparrows of Far East

(e) A Bibliography of history of education in USA

(f) How to live happily in old age

(g) Arab children

(h) Punjabi children

(i) A Biographical directory of famous Jew women

(j) Collection of Autographs of great economists

(k) Design of the London Bridge

(l) Atlas of Bridges in New York City

(m) Handbook of Vitamins

(n) Political conditions in Eastern Europe

(o) Sphinxes of Egypt.

APPENDIX

EXTENT OF SPECIFICITY

Specific means that level and scope which indicates exactly and succinctly the subject of the document. A book on Roses is entered under *Roses*, not under *Flowers*. This was C.A. Cutter's rule which is being followed since. In the words of S.R. Ranganathan the subject heading should be coextensive with the thought contents of the document: "Coextensive means exact and equal representation or with equal connotations". Specific subject can be determined only on subject analysis.

There may be a question as to whether it will be of any use to be too specific. Will it not be more useful, convenient and handy to enter capsicums or gourds under the generic heading vegetables? By individual and specific entry all the vegetables will get scattered so much so that there may not be any entry under vegetables!

The answer is two fold: first, the Sears as well as the principles of direct and specific entry mandate that entry be made under the specific name and not under the class to which it belongs. But this principle is not without ambiguity. How much specific is the question. A book on heart attack could be assigned any of the SHs: Cardiovascular systems, CardioVascular disorders, Heart attack, Cerebral Thromboses. The answer depends upon library policy on specificity, which in turn is usually based on the level of library users and strength of reading material in a particular subject area. In an agriculture library it will be advisable to index under the names of individual vegetables such as potatoes, capsicum or even under their species. Similarly, in a medical library it will be useful to use headings up to the level of Cerebral Thromboses or Coronary Thromboses. In a general small public library the term may be Gynecology or Women Diseases, but in a special library it will be necessary to individually name each and every women disease.

Part of the answer may also depend whether subject headings are being applied to macro documents arranged on the shelves by some class numbers or to a micro literature stored electronically or in form of clippings or pamphlets stored in boxes. Above all the Sears has some policy limitations as stated: “The purpose of subject headings is to draw similar works together rather than to describe each one individually”.

Sears-16, p. xxxii.

8

SUBDIVISIONS

Any subject heading in the *Sears List* may be further subdivided by a variety of subdivisions shown by a dash. *For example:*

Science – Philosophy
Mathematics – Dictionaries
Economics – Bibliography
Political science – Terminology
Girls – Education
Automobiles – Brakes
Statistics – Graphic methods
Trees – India
India – History, 1857-1947
World politics – 1991-
Indian Ocean – Geography

Subdivisions of a heading violate the principle of direct and specific entry in same cases ;

United States–History–1755-1763, French and Indian War
Instead of *French and Indian War*

United States – History – 1861-1865, Civil War
Instead of *American Civil War*

But these are essentials to clearly restrict a vague heading, to make a heading more precise, and to keep related aspects together instead of scattering them. Subdivisions may broadly be divided into three categories.

1. Subdivisions of general applicability–commonly used subdivisions.

2. Subdivisions special to a given topic – topical Subdivisions
3. Subdivisions used on instructions, *e.g.*, Geographical Subdivisions.

Subdivisions of General applicability

There are certain categories of Subdivisions which can be used with any subject heading, *for example*, Terminology, Encyclopaedias, Library resources, History, Experiments, and suchlike. In the *Sears List* such Subdivisions are listed once for all in the beginning under the heading *Commonly Used Subdivisions.* These listed Subdivisions can be freely used to subdivide any heading obtained from the list – *i.e.* whether listed or coined on instructions. These Subdivisions are quite analogous to the standard Subdivisions of the DDC or common auxiliaries of the UDC. These Subdivisions represent the documentary forms, *e.g.* Periodicals, Audiovisual aids, Directories, Pictorial works, or viewpoint of presentation *viz.* Philosophy, Theory, History, Public opinion, type of material such as Dictionaries, Obituaries, Anecdotes, Bibliographies, Library resources; or specialised aspects *e.g.* Accidents, Accounting, Monuments. The list is rather varied and defies complete categorisation. The long list of 238 Subdivisions has been given on pages xii - xliii (Sears-16) in alphabetical order. This is a mixbag of bibliographical and documentary forms, viewpoint of presentation and topical Subdivisions. Though technically these can be attached to any subject headings, yet semantically many such Subdivisions, will result in absurd and nonsense combination in some cases *e.g.*

Acronyms – Dictionaries

is meaningful but

Acronym – Accidents

is meaningless, though accidents appears in the list of Commonly used Subdivisions.

Some more examples of absurd results are :

Automobiles – Censorship
Automobiles – Diseases and pests
Automobiles – Medical care
Automobiles – Religious aspects

But the following combinations are quite meaningful

Motion pictures – Censorship
Wheat – Diseases and pests
Infants – Medical care
Folk art – Religious aspects

Some of the commonly used subdivisions of limited applicability are

Accidents
Assassination
Care and hygiene
Conservation and restoration
Costumes
Drug use
Environmental aspects
Housing
Intellectual life
Medical care
Thermodynamics
Toxicology
Voyages and travels

Hence, some are of general applications namely documentary forms; others are of limited applications, *e.g.* Accidents, Anatomy, Repairing, and Waste disposal. Commonly used subdivisions are applicable to a SH of any specificity.

Education – Bibliography
Education – Aims and objectives – Bibliography
Education and state – Bibliography
Education – India – Bibliography.

(under education we are instructed to divide geographically).

These subdivisions are also applicable to any heading that can be coined according to rules :

Automobiles – Exhibitions
Ford automobiles – Exhibitions
Electric automobiles – Exhibitions

The SH Ford automobiles and Electric automobiles have been formed as per instructions under the entry Automobiles. Similarly

BMW automobiles – Exhibitions
BMW automobiles – Testing

Testing is a commonly used subdivision
Similarly we can have

BMW automobiles – Maintenance and repair
BMW automobiles – Design
BMW automobiles – Brakes
BMW automobiles – Maintenance and repair–Cost

Here cost is a commonly used subdivision

In the editions prior to the 12th edition the commonly used subdivisions were appended with scope notes specifying their probable area of application. In the present edition this has been left to the discretion and judgement of the cataloguer.

To avoid absurd and meaningless combination now there is a double entry for each of the commonly use subdivision.

1. Listed separately, pp. xii - xiv (Sears - 16).
2. Listed as an entry in the main list. Some of such entries are also used as SH *per se*, while others, as per instructions, are only to be used as a subdivision.

In the *List* under all such entries there is a specific and clear instruction to use that as a subdivision under the specified class of subjects. *For example*,

Bibliography appears in the List of commonly used subdivisions, as well as in the main list. In the main entry it is:

Bibliography 010

SA subjects and names of persons and places with the Subdivision *Bibliography, e.g. Agriculture–Bibliography; Shakespeare, William, 1564-1616 – Bibliography, United States – Bibliography.*

So the subdivision *Bibliography* could be applied through the separated list or through the main list; instructions in the list define its area of application quite precisely and clearly.

As a spin off advantage of the double entry of the commonly used subdivisions two such subdivisions may be used simultaneously : one as instructed in the main list; the other taken from the separated list. Normally only one commonly used subdivision is allowed :

Economics of moon exploration.

We look under either *moon* or even under *Exploration* to get the heading :

Moon – Exploration – Economic aspects

Costs of Antarctica exploration

Antarctica – Exploration – Costs

Here *Exploration, Economic aspects*, and *Costs* are commonly used subdivisions, and have been used simultaneously. Similarly,

Elderly - Alcoholism.
Elderly women - Europe - Alcoholism

Let us have another example *Accounting*. It occurs both as a preferred heading in the main list and as a commonly used subdivision. In the main list it is :

Accounting 657

UF Financial accounting
SA Types of industries, professions, etc. with the

subdivision *Accounting* to be added as needed.

It means that the normal area of applications the subdivision *Accounting* is professions and industries:

Automobile industries – Accounting
Defence industry – Accounting
Iron industries – Accounting
Service industries – Accounting
Librarians – Accounting

This double entry also poses the question as to when a subject say *Accounting*, or *Accident*, or *Bibliography* is to be used as a lead heading, and when it is to be used as a subdivision. The answer is easy and difficult, both. It will require judgement though not very subtle. If it is an aspect of a subject then it will be a subdivision rather than the main heading. It will be the main heading if it is a sole word. *For example*, in statistics or theory of statistics, statistics is the main heading. But in Banking statistics; population statistics, *statistics* is the subdivision being aspect of *Banking* and *population* which are the main subjects. As another example, a book on the science or theory of accounting will get the SH *Accounting*, while in 'Accounting in computer industry' accounting will be used as a subdivision of the main topic computer industry. (Kaiser's Concrete – Abstract formula is quite valid in Sears).

Sometimes both the components may seem of equal weightage *e.g.* in Automobile design and constructions. Here Kaiser's Entity Process formula may help to solve the problem. Anyway the coordination between SA instructions in the main headings and the separate list of commonly used subdivisions always leads to the same result. *For example*, while looking under *Automobile* in the main list we find Design and construction as a subdivision. When we look under *Design and construction* in the main list we are instructed that it is not used as the main heading but only as a subdivision for types of objects, structures, machines, equipments, etc. here an example of *Airplane – Design and construction* has been given by way of illustration. By any of the approach we arrive at the correctly structured heading. Double listing of the commonly used subdivisions makes it quite easy and mechanical to identify, locate and use them precisely and accurately. Nevertheless, it is always advantageous to go through the list and keep in mind the commonly used subdivisions of wide diversity. It will add to the efficiency of the cataloguers.

Enumerated Subdivisions in the List

Many SHs in the *List* have been divided topically in the list itself. These subdivisions are obviously based on the literary warrant. Such subdivisions are given under a heading to which these are specific, though may not be totally exclusive, *e.g.,* World War, 1939-1945 - Food supply. These subdivisions apply to the heading, to its derivatives, and to its broader class. These are analogous to the special auxiliaries of the UDC. *For example*:

Cancer – Chemotherapy
Cancer – Diet therapy
Cancer – Nursing
Cancer – Patients
Cancer – Chemotherapy – Research

In the latter case Research is a commonly used subdivisions. All these are enumerated headings.

These subdivisions, namely *Chemotherapy*, *Diet therapy* *Nursing* and *Patients* are also applicable to headings derived from the SH *Cancer* as instructed under SA "types of cancers to be added as needed". So we may have heading like

Breast cancer – Chemotherapy
Breast cancer – Patients – Case studies
Blood cancer – Chemotherapy
Blood cancer – Chemotherapy – Research

Research and *Case studies* are commonly used subdivisions.

These subdivisions are equally applicable to the class diseases of which cancer is a kind. So we may have headings like

Diseases – Chemotherapy
Diseases – Diet therapy
Diseases – Nursing
Diseases – Surgery
Diseases – Surgery – Research

It may be noted that *Surgery* is listed both as a topical subdivision and a commonly used subdivision.
Similarly

All the subdivisions listed under the key headings are applicable to their corresponding heading. *For example:*

English language – Alphabet
English language – Dictionaries – French
English language – Grammar
English language – Jargon

So the corresponding headings for say Hindi will be:

Hindi language – Alphabet
Hindi language – Dictionaries – Urdu
Hindi language – Dictionaries – Tamil
Hindi language – Grammar
Hindi language – Jargon

In this edition the number of topical subdivisions has been reduced, with a view to make them of general applicability. However, in cases based on literary warrant, commonly used subdivisions is also enumerated as a local/topical subdivision. *For example*, in case of "Protection" Birds–Protection is an enumerated heading, though protection is also given as a subdivision. Protection of birds is an important topic with literary warrant.

It is simply a reminder of an apt application of general heading.

Since "Birds" is also divisible geographically, so we may

have headings like

Birds – India – Protection

This is only possible if protection is given as a commonly used subdivision.

Subdivisions on Instructions

Under many headings, both preferred and non-preferred, there are instructions to use a particular heading as a subdivision.

However, the important among instructed subdivisions is the subdivision by geographical area. *For example*

Catholic Church (May subdiv. geog.)

It is a permission to subdivide the heading geographically by place, region, country, state or city:

It means that the SH Catholic Church may be divided by geographical area, *e.g.*

Catholic Church – Asia
Catholic Church – India
Catholic Church – Kerala
Catholic Church – Calcutta
Catholic Church – Developing Countries

Police (may subdiv. geo.) *363.2*

Police – Asia
Police – West Asia
Police – Iran
Police – Tehran

Similarly

Catholic Church – Foreign relations (May subdiv. Geog.)

Following this instruction we may coin SHs like:

Catholic Church – Foreign relations – Russia
Catholic Church – Foreign relations – India
Catholic Church – Foreign relations – Islamic countries
Catholic Church – Foreign relations – Developing countries

The scope note allows subdivisions by various political bodies, so we may have SHs like:

Catholic Church –Foreign relations –Amnesty International
Catholic Church – Foreign relations –United Nations Organisation
Catholic Church – Foreign relations – Church of England

In this case as per further (and unique) instructions "When the heading is subdivided geographically an additional entry is provided with the Catholic Church and the place in reversed positions". It means we will have to provide additional headings:

Russia – Foreign relations – Catholic Church
India – Foreign relations – Catholic Church

And also the heading like:

Amnesty International – Foreign relations
– Church of England

United Nations Organisation – Foreign relations
– Church of England

Headings Used as Subdivisions : On instruction. These are topical subdivisions. Some headings both in the categories of preferred and non-preferred headings are used as subdivisions of a class of headings. When a term is to be used as a subdivision clear instructions exist there to do so alongwith an illustration.

Exploration 910.9

SA names of celestial bodies, Continents, Regions, Countries, States, etc. with the subdivision *Exploration* for materials on the Exploration of these areas... *e.g. America - Exploration*

On this clear instruction and example we can have headings like:

Mars – Exploration
Moon – Exploration
Outer space – Exploration

Antarctica – Exploration
Africa – Exploration

But at the same time the Sears also lists:

Underwater exploration

Here exploration is not a subdivision.
Take an example

Photographs of Exploration of the moon
Moon – Exploration – Pictorial works

Pictorial works is a commonly used subdivision for photographs
Take another example

Quality control

SA Industries, processes, and materials with the subdivision *Quality control* to be added as needed.
On this instruction we may have SHs like:

Pumping machinery – Quality control
Library technical processes – Quality control
Paper making – Quality control
Fermentation – Quality control
Building materials – Quality control
Industries – United States – Quality Control
(For Quality control in US industries).

Take another heading:

Indians of North America – Industries – Quality control – Case studies
(Here *case studies* is a commonly used subdivision).

There are some entries in the *List* which are only used as a subdivision. *For example*:

Description

Use names of cities (except extinct cities)

countries, states and regions with the subdivision *Description, e.g.* Chicago (Ill) – Description; *United States – Description*; etc. for descriptive materials and accounts of travels..........

So we may have SHs like

Mumbai – Description
Mumbai – Description – Poetry
(For A poetic description of Mumbai; Here *Poetry* is a commonly used subdivision)

Design and construction is another such entry in the *Sears List* to be used as a subdivision only for "Types of objects, structures, machines, equipment, etc. and types of educational tests and examinations"
Example cited here is Airplanes – *Design and construction*.
On this instruction we can have SHs like:

Automobiles – Design and construction
Automobiles – Design and construction – Cost
Warships – Design and construction – Research
Robots – Design and construction
Engines – Design and construction

Prefabricated buildings – Design and construction. Cost and research are commonly used subdivisions.

Chronological Subdivisions

The commonly used subdivision History is usually divided by chronological periods. Clear span of years follows the subdivisions *History* separated by a dash. The initial and terminal years in the span are joined by a hyphen

Science – History – 1642-1978
Science – History – 1800-1899
(For History of Science in 19th Century)
Science – History – 0-1500
(For History of Science up to the Medieval times)
American Library Association – History – 1876-1976

If that period has a particular name in the history, the standardised name must follow the period

United States – History – 1600-1775, Colonial period

History of Quit India Movement, 1942
India – History – 1942, Quit India Movement

Similarly

India – History – 1857-1947, Struggle for freedom
Japan – History – 1945-1952, Allied occupation

There are also some occasions when a time period is directly attached to a heading, *e.g.*

Modern art – 1900-1999 (20th century)
Modern history – 1900-1999 (20th century)
World politics – 1945-1991
World politics – 1995-

The period following a personal name, *e.g.* Shakespeare, William, 1564-1616 is not really a chronological subdivision, but an individualising element to differentiate one name from other to avoid homonyms. So is the case with World War, 1939-1945.

Summary

A SH in the *Sears List* may further be subdivided by three types of subdivisions:

(1) Commonly used subdivisions: These are listed separately once for all and may be applied to any heading wherever required. As a new feature these are also listed in the main body of the List at appropriate places. In the main list scope of each subdivision has been explained to arrive at meaningful subdivisions of a SH. This feature helps in the use of two commonly used subdivisions at a time.

Physics – Experiments – Bibliography. These commonly used subdivisions include documentary forms such as dictionaries, periodicals; types of material such as statistics, bibliographies, maps, data; or viewpoint such as history, philosophy, theory. These also include topical subdivisions such as costs, economic aspects, environmental aspects.

The other kinds of subdivisions are obtained by instructions at appropriate places. Prominent among such instructions is division by geographical area given by the parenthetical instructions ("May subdiv. geog.)".

Civil services – India
Civil services – Rajasthan

The third category belongs to some non-geographical headings used on instructions. *For example*, under the heading *Awards* we are instructed to use this heading as a subdivision for awards in subjects, corporate bodies, etc. *For example*, Science – Awards; Books – Awards; American Library Association – Awards. Similarly Education is also used as a subdivision for some classes of person, *e.g. Women – Education*; Blind – Education. Some entries in the list are exclusively used as subdivisions, for example, *Design and construction* to be used with types of objects, machines, equipment: *Buildings – Design and construction.* Chronological subdivisions are mostly used with the subdivisions History Politics and Arts. It means these are subdivisions of a subdivision *i.e.* secondary subdivisions, *e.g.* Japan – *History – 1945-1952, Allied occupation.*

These subdivisions make a vague subject heading quite specific and precise and bring together all aspects of a topic.

Exercise

Find the subject heading for:

1. Encyclopaedia of Philosophy
2. Bibliography of encyclopaedias of Philosophy
3. Dictionary of Encyclopaedias
4. Handbook of Dictionaries
5. Philosophy of Education: A quarterly journal
6. Indian Philosophy of Education
7. A pictorial history of India from 1942 to 1947.
8. Television law in Pakistan

9. Quotations on courage
10. Library resources on women employment
11. Registers of Indian Army
12. Register of Refugees of the Indo-Pak War of 1971.
13. A Catalogue of Medical Journals.
14. Design of Aeroplanes
15. Awards in Chemistry.

9

GEOGRAPHICAL HEADINGS AND SUBDIVISIONS

A Geographic entity of any feature or vastness *e.g.* Europe, Eastern Europe, Poland, British Commonwealth, West Indies, Baltic States, SAARC countries, Indian Ocean, Gobi Desert, Cape Comorin, Himalayan region, Peak K2, forms both a subject heading as well as a subdivision of a heading. In titles like European history, Indian history, Government of Pakistan, Churches in London or Rivers in Europe, or Avifauna of the Scandinavia, mention of geographical areas in their subject headings seems very essential.

A geographic place could be a heading *i.e.* entry element; or it could be a subdivision. In other words there are no clear rules on whether to subdivide a subject by place; or to subdivide a geographic entity by topic. Broadly speaking in the fields of science, technology and economics, geographical place is a subdivision of the topic. Whereas in subjects of history, geography, politics, culture and other aspects of social studies the geographic place itself forms the heading, with further topical subdivisions. Nevertheless it has been warned that "there are no definite rules on whether to subdivide by place or by subject" (Principles, Sears-16, p. xxv).

Names of places as follow are among the categories of headings to be added by the cataloguer (Sears-16, p. xxxxix):

(a) *Political units* : countries, states, cities, provinces, counties, dlstricts etc.

(b) *Groups of states or countries or political unions e.g:* Southern States, Baltic States, Soviet Union, Latin

America, NATO Countries, European Union, SAARC, G-8, OPECs.

(c) *Geographic features :* Names of mountain ranges and individual mountains, Island groups, and individual Islands, rivers valleys and individual rivers, seas, oceans, lakes, deltas, forests, capes, bays, deserts, canyons, marshes etc.

Related topics to be supplied by the cataloguers are names of nationalities such as Indians, Lapps, Nepalis, Africans.

In case of political and administrative units of a geographical entity, the key headings are : *United States* (for a country). *Ohio* (for a state/province) and *Chicago* (Ill) for a city. Topical subdivisions under these are applicable to any countries, city or state. *For example*, take the title:

A Demographic study of Malaysia

Since this heading pertains to a country, we will look under the heading *United States* and scan its subdivisions. There is no heading such as United States – Demography. Then we look for the topical heading, *viz.*, Demography (p. 206). There we are directed to use *Population.* Again going back to the heading United States we find the heading

United States – Population

Therefore our appropriate heading got by substituting Malaysia for United States is

Malaysia – Population

This may further be subdivided by a commonly used subdivision, if needed *e.g.*

Population atlas of India

Here Atlas a common subdivision, our apt heading thus will be :

India - Population - Atlas

Similarly, Fodder's Guide to India

India – Guidebooks

Boundaries of China will get the SH :

China – Boundaries

Similarly statistics of population of Japan, will get the SH :

Japan – Population – Statistics

Population laws of China, will get the SH

China – Population – Law and legislation.

National Institution and Organisations

In case of national organisation and institutions the Sears follows the Anglo-American Cataloguing Rules, 2nd ed. (AACR–2). Let us take a title :

History of Parliament of India

Looking under the United States we have the corresponding heading.

United States. Congress

Therefore, our SH will be:

India. Parliament – History

Lower House of Indian Parliament will get the SH:

India. Parliament. Lok Sabha

Its Upper House will get the SH

India. Parliament. Rajya Sabha

Similarly, Recruitment procedure in the Pakistani army will get the SH.

Pakistan. Army – Recruitment, enlistment, etc.

Headings for States/Provinces

For any state *Ohio* is the key heading with all its topical subdivisions.

Climate of New South Wales

Since it pertains to a state/province (of Australia), our model heading is Ohio. There the topical heading is *Ohio–climate*. Therefore, our heading is :

New South Wales – Climate

Let us take another title:

A tourist guide to Goa

Since Goa is a state so looking under Ohio we see *Description and travel.* This is a non–preferred heading and we are directed to: *Ohio–Description*. But it is a peculiar case as the common subdivision "Guidebook" is not to be added directly to this heading but to a modified heading. That is to from "Ohio–Description – Guidebook" we are referred to:

Ohio – Guidebooks

Replacing Ohio by Goa we get the desired SH:

Goa – Guidebooks

Let us take, History societies of Rajasthan

Looking under Ohio, and substituting Ohio by Rajasthan, we get

Rajasthan – History – Societies

However, a specific organisation say "Rajasthan History Association" will get SH as such being a specific name of an organisation.

Similarly, Library associations of Haryana will get the SH.

Haryana – Library – Societies

But "Haryana Library Association" will get the SH as such *i.e.* Haryana Library Association.

Let us take another title "A handbook of the Economy of Assam ". Its SH will be:

Assam – Economic conditions – Handbooks, manuals, etc.

Statistics of Tamil Nadu.

Tamil Nadu – Statistics

SHs for Cities and Towns

For a city/town the key heading is Chicago (Ill). Parenthetical qualifier "Ill" is the abbreviation for Illinois state to which Chicago belongs. If redundant this qualifier may be dropped in case of other countries.

A traveller's guide to Bombay
We will look under Chicago (Ill) to coin

Mumbai – Guidebooks

(Mumbai is the latest current name for erstwhile Bombay)
Similarly, Map of Madras

Chennai – Maps

A study of the census and commerce of Karachi.

Karachi – Census
Karachi – Commerce

A guide to industries in Manchester
Manchester – Industries – Guidebook

Simultaneous use of two Geographic Areas in a SH

When two geographic areas are related together in context of a subject, such as in foreign relations, commercial relations between two countries or regions, then there is provision in the Sears to join together two such areas. *For example*, India's Foreign Policy towards Pakistan. We look under United States to get the following SH

United States – Foreign relations (May subdiv. Geog.)

So our subject heading will be

India – Foreign relations – Pakistan

There is an instruction to permute such heading to get, *e.g.*

Pakistan – Foreign relations – India

Similarly, we may have SHs like.

India – Foreign relations – Arab countries.

Another such provision occurs for Commercial relations between two countries. There we can have SHs like

China – Commerce – United States

For Sino–US commerce. This is as per instructions given under the SH **International Trade** (p. 389) and also under **Commerce** (p. 163).

Geographical Areas as a Subdivision

As already said the rules whether a geographical area will be a heading or a subdivision are hazy:

> Note that in certain cases there are no definite rules on whether to subdivide a SH by place or divide area by subject. In general, subject headings in the fields of science, technology, economics, education and the arts are subdivisions by place, while aspects of History, Geography and Politics are subdivided by place. In many of the social sciences, the aspect of the subject that is more important or the primary focus is the criterion for decision. A work on social life and customs, *for example*, is likely to be about the social life and customs of a particular place *e.g.* **United States – Social Life and Customs**. Single parent family on the other hand, is a subject of general interest and is only secondarily about single parent families in a particular place. (Even though it is not subdivided by place in Sears **Single parent family** may nonetheless be subdivided geographically if the material in a given library warrants) (Sears–16, p. xxv).

It means SHs in the field of science, technology, economics, education and arts are divided by place:

Science – India
Industrial policy – China
Flowers – Finland
Flowers – Helsinki
Archives – Calcutta
Museums – West Bengal

In history, geography and politics the geographic place name should act as a SH with topical subdivisions taken from the key headings:

Tamil Nadu – Geography
Karnataka – Politics and government
Andhra Pradesh – Social conditions
Developing countries – Commerce

In most cases the common sense rule is to bring to the forefront the most important component or the focus of the subject in a compound or subdivided SH.

When a subject heading is not found under a geographical key heading, it is advisable to look under the topic itself. Under that subject there may be instructions to subdivide that SH geographically.

In the Sears many headings are divisible by geographic area. All such headings are appended with the instruction in parenthesis: "(May subdiv. Geog.)" – which means "may be subdivided geographically".

The geographic unit used as subdivision may be a region, country, state or city: *For example*

Intellectuals (May subdiv. Geog.)

Subject headings that may be coined from this heading can be:

Intellectuals – Greece
Intellectuals – Ontario
Intellectuals – Mumbai
Intellectuals – Mumbai – Biography
Intellectuals – Arab Countries
Intellectuals – G-8
Intellectuals – West Asia
Intellectuals – British Commonwealth
Intellectuals – Developing Countries

Take some other examples of the SHs to be divided geographically:

Libraries (may subdiv. Geog.) 027

We can have headings like:

Libraries – Europe – Directories
Libraries – Scandinavia – Biography
Libraries – Central Europe
Libraries – Frankfurt
Libraries – SAARC countries

Libraries – India
Libraries – Gujarat
Women – Himalayan states
Women – Assam
Women – Guwahati
Holidays – Varanasi – Government policy
Trees – Hyderabad (Pakistan).

(Here Hyderabad city needs to be qualified by country as there are two cities named Hyderabad – one in India and other in Pakistan.

Political parties (p. 560) may be subdivided geographically *e.g.*

Political parties – India
Political parties – Jammu and Kashmir

However, an individual political party will be entered directly under is own name

Nepali Congress
Communist Party of India (Marxist)
Indian National Congress(I) – History – 1885-1985.
Bhartiya Janata Party – Biography
(For who's who of Bhartiya Janata Party).
Nepali Congress – Philosophy

History, Biography and Philosophies, are commonly used subdivisions. Take another example

Extinct cities – Greece – Atlases
Extinct cities – India – Maps
Extinct cities – Research

Take another example

Gardens (May subdiv. Geog.) 635; 712

Gardens of **Mysore** city

Gardens – Mysore
Atlas of English Gardens
Gardens – England – Atlas

However, a specific garden will be entered under its own name, *e.g.*

Brindaban Gardens Mysore, will get the SH
Brindaban Gardens

Similarly, A guide to Lalbagh of Bangalore will get the SH

Lalbagh Garden – Guidebook
A history of Shalimar Garden (Srinagar)
Shalimar Garden – History

Similarly, sanctuaries, parks, resorts, hotels, monuments will be entered under their own specific names. *For example*

Taj Mahal – History
Taj Mahal – Architecture

Restricted Geographical Areas

In some cases, range of area to be used as a subdivision is limited or specified. *For example,*

Blacks (may be subdivided geog. except US) 305.896.

From the above instruction it is clear that the SH Blacks may be divided by any area other than US). So we have :

Blacks – Europe
Blacks – London
Blacks – Canada
Blacks – South America

Since US Blacks are known as African Americans so aptly a heading like Blacks – United States has not been allowed. We will have to make a see cross reference

Blacks – United States
See African Americans

Take another example

Americans (may subdivid. Geog. except US) 305.843; 920; 973

Scope note lays down that it is to be used for documents on US citizen.

We can have headings like

Americans – Europe
Americans – Central Europe
Americans – Scandinavia
Americans – Germany
Americans – Arab countries
Americans – Developing countries
Americans – Iberia

Above SHs are for US citizens residing in these regions. On the analogy we can divide national groups by regions *e.g.*

Japanese – United States
(which is different from Japanese Americans)
Pakistanis – Arab countries
Nepalese – India
Sri Lankans – Europe

(Mexicans – United states is different from Mexican Americans – the latter are naturalised US citizens).

American literature (may subdiv. geog. by state or region) 810.

Obviously a SH like American literature – United States will be absurd. But division by US states or regions has been permitted.

American literature – Taxas
American literature – New England
American literature – Virgin Islands
American literature – Northern states

On this analogy we can have SHs

Hindi literature – Rajasthan
For Rajasthani Hindi literature

Hindi literature – Punjab
(for Hindi literature published from Punjab)

Similarly we can have

Punjabi literature – Jammu and Kashmir

Punjabi literature – Delhi
Punjabi literature – India
Punjabi literature – Pakistan

Even a heading already subdivided topically may be further divided geographically, *e.g.*

Jews – Persecution (may sub div. Geog. 909; 933)

Here we can have such headings as

Jews – Persecution – Europe
Jews – Persecution – Germany

Nations in Adjectival forms in Subject Headings

Some countries/nations, especially in subjects of culture are now used in adjectival form, *e.g.*

Scottish personal names
American sculpture
Greek sculpture
American artificial satellites
Scandinavian literature
Icelandic literature
Indian literature

On the analogy of American artificial satellites we can form a heading Indian artificial satellites for the Insat and Rohini. Now question arises as to how to judge whether a given heading will be in the adjectival national form or in a noun form. For such headings the usual instruction is given under the general heading against the SA (see also) legend, *e.g.*

Personal Names (may subdiv geog.) 929.4

SA personal names of particular national or ethnic origins regardless of the place when they are found, *e.g.* Scottish personal names to be added as needed.
On this analogy we may have SHs like

Finnish personal names
Indian personal names
Assamese personal names

Bengali personal names
North Indian personal names
Punjabi personal names
Sindhi personal names
South Indian personal names
Tamil personal names

On this analogy we may coin and add SHs for Indian (Asian) ethnic names

Marwarhi personal names
Sikh personal names
Naga personal names
Manipuri personal names

Similarly under

Art 700

SA; and art of particular countries for regions, *e.g.* Greek art, to be added as needed.
On this instruction we can have headings like

Asian art
Greek art
French art

Similarly as per SA instruction under *Architecture* we may have headings like

Renaissance architecture
American architecture
Byzantine architecture
Greek architecture
Roman architecture
Mughal architecture
Victorian architecture

The Sears, being meant for small libraries does not distinguish between French art, and Art – France. But it has been permitted in the 'Principles' (Sears 16, p. xxix) that if warranted by strength of material and ratified by a written policy both the headings can be established and used properly distinguishing between the two *i.e.* **Art – France** may not necessarily be all French arts whereas **French Art** may also be found in, say, Germany or Africa. It means that national arts/architecture (in adjectival form) may further be subdivided by country.

Victorian architecture – India
French Art – India
Indian Art – France
Chinese art – Europe
Japanese art – London – Exhibitions
Asian art – Europe – Study and teaching

Take another example

Artists 709.2; 920

SA artist of particular countries, *e.g.* American artists

So on this instruction and example we have SHs like

African American artists
Indian artists
German artists
German artists – Biography
Diaries of artists of Finland
Finnish artists – Diaries

Direct and Indirect Geographical Subdivisions

There arises a vital question of direct or indirect form of a geographic subdivision. Direct form means a place name is used directly to divide a heading. *For example*

Holidays – Varanasi

It is a direct geographic subdivision. But if greater geographic regions(s) is/are interposed then it is called indirect subdivision. *For example*, the above heading could be transcribed as

Holidays – India – Uttar Pradesh – Varanasi

The Sears prefers direct form (p. xxiv) in accordance wlth its policy principle of direct and specific entry. But if a library wants to show the subject catalogue displayed in a systematic hierarchy *i.e.* logical collocation of broader and its narrower areas then it is essential to use the geographic subdivisions indirectly. Indirect headings are especially useful in bibliographies. For computerised storage and retrieval indirect form holds many potential uses as the search can be formulated up or down the hierarchy; and of course it is equally useful for browsing and freetext searching. Collocation of related material is the main and clear advantage. *For example*

Libraries – India
Libraries – India – Gujarat
Libraries – India – Gujarat – Ahmedabad
Libraries – India – Gujarat – Baroda
Libraries – India – Gujarat – Surat
Libraries – India – Gujarat – Bhavnagar

Obviously all the entries on libraries in different cities of Gujarat state will be displayed together in a catalogue or bibliography, whereas in a direct form these will get scattered alphabetically.

Similarly,

Holidays – India – Uttar Pradesh
Holidays – India – Uttar Pradesh – Haridwar
Holidays – India – Uttar Pradesh – Lucknow
Holidays – India – Uttar Pradesh – Varanasi

Such a catalogue is called Alphabetic – classed catalogue.

Here another important question arises as to how much indirect a heading should be?

For example, the above two headings could also be transcribed as:

Libraries – South Asia–India–West India–Gujarat – Ahmedabad

And

Holiday–South Asia–India–North India – Uttar Pradesh–Haridwar

The answer is subjective and local–on which region you wish to collocate the material. In the above example we will have collection by South Asia, then by country and so on.

Geography as a Subdivision

Of allied interest is the term geography used as a subdivision.

Geography 910

Materials limited to a particular place are entered under the name of the place with the subdivision *Geography.*

SA names of countries, states, etc. with the subdivision *Description* and *Geography*; and sacred works with the subdivision Geography, *e.g.* Bible – Geography to be added as needed.

On this instruction and example we may have SHs like:

Europe – Geography
South Asia – Geography
India – Geography
Western Ghat – Geography

These headings may, of course be further subdivided if needed, by any of the commonly used subdivisions.

Europe – Geography – Dictionaries
South East Asia – Geography – Congresses
Western Ghats – Geography – Pictorial works

Further headings for Geography as depicted in sacred works may be

Old Testament – Geography
Vedas – Geography – Atlas
Ramayana – Geography – Dictionaries

Option

It may be noted that parenthetical instruction to subdivide geographically is permissive not mandatory (p. xxivi, Sears– 16).

It has been further allowed that even if not instructed, subject heading may be subdivided geographically.

Furthermore, if a library prefers geographic subdivision for subjects that are not so indicated in the Sears the library should feel free to add them (p. xxiv, Sears – 16).

This should be done only on formulating a definite and recorded policy.

Some Relevant Commonly Used Subdivisions

Some of the commonly used subdivisions and SHs closely related to geographical works are:

Atlases
Description
Exploration
Gazetteers
Geographical distributions
Maps
Travel
Travellers
Underwater exploration
Voyages and travels

Summary

A geographical entity, such as geographic place or feature form both a heading as well as a subdivision of a topic. Subjects in the field of science, technology, economics, education, arts, etc. are divided by place; while aspects of history geography, politics are subdivisions of a place. The rules are hazy and fuzzy. As a general rule aspect of a compound subject that is more prominent will form the lead heading and the other component is relegated as subdivision. When a country, state or city is the heading the topic subdivision are to be obtained from the key headings namely **United States**, **Ohio** and **Chicago** (Ill.) respectively.

All the SHs in the Sears divisible by a geographical place

are indicated so; '(may subdiv. geog.)'. It means the given heading may be subdivided by geographical area of any extent unless specified otherwise. In case of a country and its organ or constitutional institutions being the subject, the SH is given the form/structure according to Anglo-American Cataloguing Rules (AACR 2) and clear examples are given under the SH **United States.** Thus we have heading such as **India. Parliament. Rajya Sabha** for Upper House of the Indian Parliament. In case of commercial relations and Foreign relations between two countries, the two areas are to be used simultaneously. *For example*, Pakistan–Foreign relations–Afghanistan; India– Foreign relations–Islamic countries. In some cases the Geographical area used as a subdivision is restricted in range as per instruction given there. *For example*, **Blacks** is divisible geographically by any area except United States, as for US Blacks the SH is African Americans. Geographical area as a subdivision may be used as direct or indirect subdivision though in principle Sears prefers direct heading or subdivisions. *For example*, Holidays – Australia – New South Wales – Sydney is indirect while Holidays – Sydney is direct subdivision. Direct subdivision is easy to search, while indirect subdivision collocates related entries together and displays them systematically. It is especially useful for bibliographies and classified catalogues. For OPACs indirect subdivisions have added advantage as the chain may be truncated at any point in searching.

In some cases, especially art and literature, nation is used in the adjectival from *e.g. Scottish personal names. American artificial satellite* and *French sculpture.* Sears being a small list does not distinguish between Greek art and Art–Greece, yet if needed both the headings may be established.

The term geography is also a subdivision for some headings such as Gobi desert–Geography, Vedas–Geography, Bible–Geography. Some closely related commonly used subdivisions are Atlases, Exploration, gazetteers, geographical distribution, maps, travels, voyages.

Exercise

1 Distinguish the cases where geographical place is a heading or a subdivision.

2 Explain the advantages and disadvantages of direct and indirect subdivisions.

3 Assign subject headings to the following topics:

a. Folksongs of Finland

b. Emperors of Japan

c. Recruitment procedure of English Royal Army

d. Biographical dictionary of Famous Men and Women of Maharashtra.

e. Pictorial guide to Cairo

f. Museums of Calcutta

g. Foreign relations between Japan and USA

h. India's Foreign Policy towards African countries

i. Tourist guide to Nepal

j. Agriculture Atlas of India

k. Nepalis in India.

10

SUBJECT HEADINGS FOR LANGUAGES AND LINGUISTICS

Subject headings for a particular language and its aspects are covered by a key heading English language. In addition, there are many independent headings for linguistics, and language as a social entity, and communication media.

Languages: For any language and or its grammatical or educational aspects English language forms the key heading:

English language 420

Subdivisions used under this heading may be used under other languages unless otherwise specified.

For this, we have only to replace the word *English* by the other language. By this permission to substitute, we may have SHs like:

Sanskrit language
Korean language
French language
Chinese language
Farsi language
Latin language

All the subdivisions given under *English language* and all the appropriate commonly used subdivisions are applicable here *e.g.*

A Sanskrit grammar, will get the SH:

Sanskrit language – Grammar

A history of Russian dialects, will get the SH: *Russian*

language–Dialects–History. Here Russian language–Dialects has been formed on the analogy of *English language–Dialects* whereas *History* is a commonly used subdivision attachable to any subject heading. Let us take a few more examples:

A study of orthography of Danish:

Danish language – spellings

Handbook on the use of foreign words in Hindi:

Hindi language – Foreign words and phrases – Handbooks, manuals, etc.

A dictionary of Swedish synonyms

Swedish language – Synonyms and antonyms – Dictionaries

Teaching English as a second language, will get the SH:

English as a second language.

There is no need to subdivide this heading by the commonly used subdivision *study and teaching* as teaching is implied in the SH itself. It is further clear from one of the UFs under this heading, *viz.* "English language–Study and teaching, Foreign".

It may also be noted that in the SH the word language does not appear. On this analogy we may have headings like:

Hindi as a second language
Urdu as a second language
Spanish as a second language

In Indian situations it may be necessary to divide above headings geographically by state:

Teaching Punjabi as a second language in Haryana State

Punjabi as a second language – Haryana

Second language status to French in Schools of Pondicherry.

French as a second language–Pondicherry.

Some more examples:

Use of Hindi for business and commerce

Hindi language–Business Hindi

Similarly we can have

Finnish language–Business Finnish

Bilingual Dictionaries

Bilingual dictionaries make another interesting case in SHs work. The key heading for such works has been given:

English language – Dictionaries – French

It is a SH for a dictionary whose words have been given in English and their equivalents or meanings are given in French.

(It will be mostly useful for French knowing people who wish to know the meaning of an English word).

Take the following entry in the Sears:

English language – Dictionaries 423

Use for English language dictionaries. Dictionaries from English to another language are entered under this heading further subdivided by the other language, *e.g.* English language–Dictionaries–French; French–Dictionaries–English. Combined English–French and French – English dictionaries are entered under both headings.

Similarly for Sanskrit – German dictionary the SH is :

Sanskrit language–Dictionaries–German

For English – Persian dictionary the SH is

English language–Dictionaries–Persian

Punjabi Russian Dictionary, the SH is

Punjabi language – Dictionaries – Russian

A bibliography of Spanish – English dictionaries will get the SH:

Spanish language–Dictionaries–English– Bibliography

Obviously, *Bibliography* is a commonly used subdivision.

A two–faced bilingual dictionary in which approach through words of both the languages is possible will be given double subject heading–one in reverse of the other ; *For example.* English–Tamil and Tamil – English dictionary will get the following two SHs:

English language – Dictionaries –Tamil
Tamil language – Dictionaries – English

Dictionaries as a Commonly Used Subdivision

Dictionaries is also a commonly used subdivision which may be used to specify any heading, particularly, groups or classes of persons, and names of places with the compound subdivision Biography – Dictionaries:

Fishes–Dictionaries
Mathematics–Dictionaries
Drama–Dictionaries
English drama–Dictionaries
Hinduism–Dictionaries
Accidents–Prevention–Dictionaries
Constitutional history–United States–Dictionaries
World War, 1939-1945–Monuments–Dictionaries
Women–Biography–Dictionaries
India–Biography–Dictionaries
Delhi–Biography–Dictionaries

Encyclopaedias and dictionaries is another heading to be used for general materials about Encyclopaedias and dictionaries, say for, *Encyclopaedia Britannica, Encyclopaedia Americana*

The subdivision *Encyclopaedia* is to be used with subjects, groups or classes of persons, and name of places with the subdivision Encyclopaedia.

McGraw Hill Encyclopaedia of Science and Technology will have the following two headings:

Science – Encyclopaedias

Technology – Encyclopaedias

We may have SHs like

Social medicine – Encyclopaedias
Social medicine – Japan – Encyclopaedias
(Since Social medicine is further divisible geographically)
India – Encyclopaedias
Hindu – Encyclopaedias
Inuit – Encyclopaedias

Some related SHs on Languages and Linguistics are :

Language and Languages
Linguistics
Grammar
Vocabulary
Phonetics
Semantics
Sociolinguistics
Bilingualism
Bilingual education
Modern languages
Whole language
Universal languages
Language arts
Esperanto
Sign language
Romance language
Programming language (Computers)

Take another *example*:

Politics of language, this will have the SH
Language and languages – Political aspects

The SH *Modern languages* may be subdivided like the heading *English language*. So we may have heading like:

Modern languages – Dictionaries
Modern languages – Study and teaching
Modern languages – Grammar – Research
Modern languages – Grammar – Study and teaching,

While *Grammar* is a topical subdivision, *Study and teaching*, *Research* are commonly used subdivisions.

Similarly, we may have

Modern languages – Alphabet – History
Modern languages – Homonyms

Language Groups and Families

Under the heading *Language and languages* we have the instruction to see also :

Names of languages and group of languages, *e.g. Scandinavian languages*....For material on the several languages spoken by a group or in a place, *e.g. Indians of North America – Languages*, *United States – Languages*, etc. to be added as needed.

Though not explicitly stated above instruction should also cover the language families such as Indo-European, Gothic, Teutonic, Celtic, Slavonic, Iranian, Semitic, Dravadian, and so on.

All these headings may be further divided as the English language:

Dravadian languages–Pronunciation
Semitic languages–Grammar–History
Dravadian languages–Idioms–Dictionaries

A study of the history of alphabets of Indo-European languages will get the SH:

Indo-European languages – Alphabets – History
Evolution of the grammar of Gothic languages:
Gothic languages–Grammar–History

A study of foreign elements in Indo-Aryan languages:
Indo-Aryan languages – Foreign words and phrases

Language as a Subdivision

Under the SH *Language and Languages*: There is an instruction to see also "disciplines, classes of persons, types of newspapers, and names of individual persons, corporate bodies and literary works entered under title with the subdivision *Language, e.g., Technology–Language; Children–Language*, etc. and names of ethnic groups or native people and countries, cities etc. with the subdivision Languages for material on several languages spoken by a group or in a place, *e.g. Indians of North America–Languages; United States–Languages*, etc. to be added as needed."

On this instruction we can have headings like:

Australia–Languages
India–Languages
Delhi–Languages
Children–Languages–Research
An atlas of languages spoken in Pakistan
Pakistan–Languages–Atlas
Here Atlas is a commonly used subdivision
Language policy of the Government of Canada
Canada–Languages–Government policy
(Here Government policy is a commonly used subdivision)

Some other headings can be coined form these instruction:

Science–Language
Mathematics–Language
Science–Language–Bibliography
David Copperfield–Language
Bible–Language–Research
Wordsworth, William, 1770–1850–Language
Lawyers–language
Teenagers–Language
American newspapers–Language
English newspapers–Language
Indians of North America–Language

A title "Language of the 20th century art: A conceptual history' will have two SHs namely:

Modern art–1900–1999 (20th century) – Language

Art–History

Thus we can coin subject headings for all individual languages, language groups and families, languages spoken in a region and for linguistic aspects of a given language, and also for linguistic aspects of a literary work or a literary author.

Summary

For linguistic works in any language the *English language* with all its listed (topical) subdivisions and commonly used subdivisions is the key heading. Simply replace "English" by the other language to get the appropriate SH. In addition language groups and families may also form SHs as instructed under the SH *Languages and languages*. For bilingual dictionaries *English language–Dictionaries–French* is the key heading. Besides this, *language* is also a subdivision for SHs of various groups of people, countries, cities, *e.g. China–Language* for different languages spoken in China, it is different from Chinese language. Relevant commonly used subdivisions are *Dictionaries, Language, Terminology. Modern languages* is another important SH which could further be divided as the English language. Interestingly enough, there is no SH as *Language* though it is an important subdivision. Language is covered by *Language and languages*, and *Linguistics.*

Exercise

Coin SHs for the following topics

1. English idioms
2. Grammar of Chinese language
3. Language policy in China
4. Russian English dictionary
5. Glossaries of Chemical terms
6. Language of Eskimos

7. An etymological study of modern languages
8. A critical study of the language of science and technology
9. A psychological study of the language used by teenagers
10. Geographic distribution of the use of English language.

11

SUBJECT HEADINGS FOR LITERATURE AND LITERARY WORKS

The works pertaining to literature broadly fall into categories:

(a) *Literary art, history and criticism*: These are general works irrespective of the language namely, literary techniques, criticism, history, and anthologies irrespective of language *e.g.* Aristotle's poetics, History of world drama, 20th century fiction; Quotation from World literature; Anthologies with a theme: Short stories about hunting.

(b) *Particular language literature*: These are works confined to a particular language literature or its aspects *e.g.* English literature, Korean literature, Greek poetry, Russian Fiction, Sanskrit plays. It may also include national literatures, *e.g.* (former) Soviet literature, Canadian literature, Indian literature, Scandinavian literature, Arabic literature. A particular language literature may further be divided broadly into two types:

   (i) Individual works, *e.g.* Shakespeare's *Hamlet*, Wordsworth's. *The prelude,* Leo Tolstoy's *War and Peace, Suitable Boy* by Vikram Seth, Homer's *Iliad,* Walt Whitman's *Leaves of Grass*. This may also include collected works of a monolingual author *e.g.* collected works of William Shakespeare; Selection from John Keats, an anthology of Emerson's Works.

   (ii) Literary history and criticism or collection of

more than one author of a particular language literature *e.g.* History of English literature, French, literary criticism, 20th century English literature; An anthology of 19th century French poetry; Collection of lyrical French poetry; A critical study of religious themes in Bengali plays; A history of 20th centuries German fiction.

Individual Works of Creative Literature

Individual works of literary creations such as plays, fiction, poetry, satire, and other major literary forms are not given any SH – and rightly so. *For example, War and Peace* by Leo Tolstoy will not have any SH; it will be misleading to give it the SH "Russian fiction"; nor Shakespeare's Hamlet will have a SH of English drama, or Elizabethan plays. To repeat, it is not only meaningless but quite misleading to assign a SH "Hindi fiction" to any of Prem Chand's works. The reason is obvious; a creative literary works has only form, not a subject, We do not read literary for factual knowledge of a subject, but for its literary pleasure, aesthetic feelings and for enrichment of inner experience and feelings. Hence an individual literary work need not be given any SH.

Individual Literary Authors

But individual literary authors, especially the prolific authors may be given SHs, especially in case of their anthologies or critical studies.

Shakespeare, William, 1564-1616

Serves as the key heading for topical subdivisions of any literary author, *e.g.*:

Collected poetical works of Guru Rabinder Nath Tagore will get the SH.

Tagore, Rabindra Nath, 1861-1941– Poetry

Study of social psychology in the works of Tagore.

Tagore, Rabindra Nath, 1861-1941 – Knowledge

– Social psychology.

The above heading has been formed on the pattern of:

Shakespeare, William, 1564-1616 – Knowledge – Animals:

(Social psychology is an independent heading in the Sears list).

A study of the characterisation of Charles Dickens.

Dickens, Charles, 1812-1870 - Characters

Poetic art of Thomas Hardy

Hardy, Thomas, 1840-1928 – Poetry

A bibliography of works on and by John Keats

Keats, John, 1792-1821 – Bibliography

A critical interpretation of the American poet Walt Whitman.

Whitman, Walt, 1819-1892–Criticism

A critical study of the style of Thomas Hardy.

Hardy, Thomas, 1840-1928–Technique

A critical study of the characters of Henry Fielding.

Fielding, Henry, 1707-1754–Characters.

Above heading can be arrived at *via* two routes. Firstly when we look under the key heading, we get a very appropriate and apt model heading:

Shakespeare, William, 1564-1616–Characters.

The second route is to look under the heading: Characters and Characterisation in literature.

Under its *see also* legend we are instructed to see also names of authors with the subdivision characters.

Subject Headings for a Literary Work

It is misleading to say that no individual literary work will have any SH. Some exceptional literary works especially based on some high historical or outstanding personality may have a SH. Fictionalised biographies, fiction on social, historical issues, Science or utopian fiction also get a SH. In such a case the literary form of the work will be subdivision of the theme of the work as the main heading.

A play on the life of Mahatma Gandhi may get the heading.

Gandhi, Mohandas Karamchand, 1869 -1948 – Drama

A novel (in any language) on the French Revolution, will get the heading.

France–History– 1789-1799, Revolution–Fiction

Collection of poems on Freedom Movement of India, will get the SH:

India – History – 1857-1947, Freedom movement – poetry.

Death – poetry is the SH for Oxford Book of Death, which is a collection of poems on death.

If it is a critical study of a historical personality treated in various works of literature then the name should be divided by the subdivision *In literature*.

Depiction of Jawaharlal Nehru in Literature:

Nehru, Jawaharlal Nehru, 1889 - 1964 – In literature

Depiction of Napolean Bonaparte in literature,

Napolean I, 1769-1821– In literature

But a novel on the life and achievements of Napolean will get.

Napolean I, 1769-1821– Fiction.

Play on Abraham Lincoln by John Drinkwater,

Lincoln, Abraham, 1809-1865 – Drama.

Treatment of Joan de Arc in French literature will get the heading (irrespective of language).

Joan, *Saint* of Arc 1412-1431 – In literature.

As an exception, the subject portrayal of women in literature will get the SH *Women in literature.*

Delhi: a novel by Khushwant Singh.

In this fictional work the history of Delhi has been traced from the ancient to the present times. It may be given the heading.

Delhi – History – Fiction.

Here Delhi – History has been obtained on the key heading of Chicago – History; and *Fiction* is a common subdivision.

A collection of stories on animal wisdom

Animal intelligence – Stories, plots, etc.

Stories about Dogs will get the SH. *Dogs – Fiction*, but a critical study in literature irrespective of languages will get the SH **Dogs in literature.**

Stories based on Mughal history of India will get the SH.

India – History–1526-1857, Mughals– Stories, plots, etc.

H.G.Well's *The Time Machine* will get the SH.

Science fiction.

George Orwell's 1984 – may be given the SH:

Utopian fiction.

Following types of literary works are given SHs

1 Anthologies of various language literatures,
2 Anthologies of works of different authors writing in the same language,
3 Literary theory, history or criticism, techniques and styles,
4 Individual prolific authors on the pattern of Shakespeare, William, 1564–1616.
5. Works in minor genre or with a dominant theme.

Same examples alongwith SHs are given below:

Specimens of World Literature

Literature – Collections.

Specimens of plays from different languages of the World.

Drama – Collections

An encyclopaedia of German literature.

German literature – Encyclopaedias (Encyclopaedia is a commonly used subdivision). Pattern for German literature has been obtained on the key heading English literature.

A treasury of Indian literature

Indian literature – Collections

Similarly, a bibliography of French poetry will get the SH

French poetry – Bibliography

A Bibliography on history of Hindi poetry will get the SH.

Hindi poetry – History and criticism – Bibliography.

For obvious reasons the heading *English literature* and for that reason 'Sanskrit literature' will never be used as such alone. These will need at least a subdivision.

English literature – Encyclopaedias
Hindi literature – Examinations

Other key headings for literary works pertaining to a particular language literature can be inferred from the legend NT of the SH *English literature* 820. On the analogy of various headings given here, SHs for other languages can be formed.

An anthology of Hindi poetry

Hindi poetry – Collections

A History of Sanskrit plays

Sanskrit drama – History and criticism.

Dramatic art of G. B . Shaw

Shaw, Goerge Bernard, 1856-1950 – Drama

Prose style of James Boswell

Boswell, James, 1740-1795 – Technique

(This has been formed on the analogy of Shakespeare, William, 1564-1616–Technique).

Some related SHs

Poetry in Indian English

Indian poetry (English)

(It has been coined on the pattern of Canadian poetry (English).

On the analogy of English authors we may have headings like.

Bengali authors
Urdu authors
Tamil authors
Hindi authors
Russian authors

(But we cannot have a heading like Canadian authors, Scandinavians author or Indian authors).

These various language authors may further be subdivided by any of the suitable commonly used subdivisions.

Directory of German authors
German authors – Directories

A social study of Bengal writers.

Bengali authors – Social conditions.

Singular or Plural Usage

It is important to understand the singular and plural forms usage of literary forms as subject headings. The differentiation is rather simple. Singular noun is used when a literary form is the subject of study; while plural form is used as a subdivision.

For example, Essay is the SH for the art and technique of essay writing or composing essays, while SH Essays is used for a collection of essays. *For example*, a book of essays by Bacon, Addision and Steele will get the heading.

Essays – Collections

Similarly, the SH Short story is used for the technique of writing short stories or short stories as a literary genre, while *Short stories* is used as a SH for a collection of Short stories by one or more authors. *For example,* O'Henry's Short stories will get a SH *Short stories.* A collection of short stories will get the SH *Short stories* as the subdivision Collection cannot be added to it. But a dictionary of short stories will get the SH.

Short stories – Dictionaries

Similarly the SH

Short stories – Technique

is not admissible though *technique* is a commonly used subdivision. Its correct SH will be simply *Short story.* As an exception SH Fiction is given to both a collection of fiction from various languages as well as the art of fiction writing.

Literary Forms

Interestingly literary forms are the SHs as well as subdivisions of a SH. In case, a literary form is the subject of study, then this will be the SH:

An encyclopaedia of world drama.

Drama – Dictionaries

Art of stage plays

Drama – Technique

How to write poems

Poetics

(This SH has been arrived at by looking under the SH poetry and its scope note. There we are directed that "Materials on the art and technique of poetry are entered under Poetics".

How to write better fiction

Fiction – Technique

Some Literary Subdivisions

Followings are the common subdivisions specific to the class literature. These have been extracted from the general list of commonly used subdivisions. It may be noted that as per the Sears-16 policy the subdivisions given under key headings have not been listed in this list of commonly used subdivisions. The following list, therefore, may be convenient and time saving as well as suggestive for subdividing literary SHs.

Indexes

Anecdotes
Bio-bibliography
Biography
Cartoons and caricatures
Collections
Compositions
Correspondence
Drama
Fiction
Folklore
History and criticism
Humour
Information services
Juvenile literature
Language
Library resources
Literary collections
Miscellanea
Obituaries
Parodies, imitations,etc.
Periodicals
Philosophy
Pictorial works.
Portraits
Posters
Programmed instructions
Prophecies
Quotations
Reviews
Songs
Stories, plots, etc.
Study and teaching
Texts

These subdivisions may be used to specify any of the headings in the list to form a suitable heading for any sort of literature in the wider sense of the term. *For example*, short stories on nuclear war.

Nuclear warfare – stories, plots, etc. It may be given another SH of Short stories which is used for collection of short stories by one or more authors.

Literary quotable quotes

Literature – Quotations

Quotable quotes from Alexander Pope, the classical poet.

Pope, Alexander, 1688-1744 – Quotations.

Syllabus for teaching Shakespeare,

Shakespeare, William, 1564-1616 – Outlines, syllabus, etc.

Texts of plays based on the Holy Bible

Bible plays–Texts

History of French literary essays

French essays–History

(French essays has been obtained on the analogy of English essays; history is a commonly used subdivision).

Summary

Subject headings for literary works is one of the problematic area which requires close analysis of the documents and close study of the Sears list. SHs for literary works are many, varied, and scattered. Broadly, we divide the works falling in the Dewey's Main Class 800 into two categories: Literary history, theory, techniques and anthologies irrespective of language; creative works of a specific language literature in any literary form such as poetry, fiction, stories, essays and many more. The literary works in the same language may be by a single author or may be a collection of works by several authors writing in same literary form, or irrespective of form.

Subject headings for collected works in any one language are coined on the model of *English literature*. Individual authors are given headings on the analogy of Shakespeare, William 1564-1616.

More importantly, individual literary works do not need any SH except in some special cases such as minor literary forms, namely, Satire, Short stories, science fiction, and works based on a, historical event or personality. *For example*, Charles Dickens' *David Copperfield* will not be given any SH. It will be misleading to give the SH English fiction to it, but HG Well's *Time Machine* may be given the SH *Science fiction* and George Orwell's 1984 may get the SH *Utopian fiction.* Also literary and fictional works on a historical event or personality may get a subject heading based on the subject subdivided by its literary form. *For example*, John Drinkwater's Cromwell will get the SH: *Cromwell, Oliver, 1599-1658 – Drama.* A SH may not usually be assigned to collected works of a single author except in case the author writes in minor literary form such as parody, satire, or are his/her speeches or diaries. *For example*, collected satirical works of Janathan Swift may get a SH *Satire* or preferably *English Satire.* Samuel Peppys' Diary may get a SH *Peppy, Samuel, 1633-1703 – Diaries.*

Other works pertaining to a language literature get SHs on the pattern of key heading English literature and its subdivisions. All narrower terms (given against NT) of this key heading provide useful clue and guidance to provide subject headings for works in literary forms of other literatures. A heading like English literature, for that reason, French literature, or Spanish literature, will never be used alone as such. These will be used in subdivided forms, *e.g.* Russian literature–Bibliography. National literature, *e.g.* Canadian litreature, American literature, Indian literature form subject headings.

Exercise

Assign subject heading to the following titles

1. An anthology of German poetry of 19th Century.
2. Vanity Fair by William Makepiece Thackery (1811-1863).
3. Short stories on hunting expeditions based in India.
4. Children stories of Rabindra Nath Tagore (1861 - 1941) Bengali Nobel Laureate.
5. Collection of Canadian short stories in Punjabi.

6. On the art of writing fiction.
7. History of American essays.
8. An anthology of French poetry.
9. Robert Browning's characters: a study.
10. A study of portrayal of Joseph Stalin in literature.(1879-1953).
11. The Sacred Wood by TS Eliot (1888 -1965)
12. R W Emerson's Essays.

Answers

1. German poetry – Collections
2. No SH will be given
3. Hunting – India – Stories, plots, etc.
4. Children's literature
5. Canadian short stories (Punjabi) (This will be formed on the basis of *Canadian poetry (English).*
6. Fiction
7. American essays–History and criticism.
8. French poetry–Collections
9. Browning, Robert, 1812-1889 –Characters.
10. Stalin, Joseph, 1879-1953 –In literature
11. Criticism .
12. American essays

12

SUBJECT HEADINGS FOR BIOGRAPHIES AND AUTOBIOGRAPHIES

Biography is a subject heading as well as a common subdivision. As a subject heading it covers material on the collection of biographies not confined to a place or class. As a commonly used subdivision it may be added to any SH in the List wherever required and appropriate. Usually it is added as a subdivision to collective biographies of persons or to an individual person's name. Another related heading with obvious meaning is *Biography as a literary* form. This heading applies only to the art or technique of biography writing. *Autobiography, and Autobiographies* are other two related headings with obvious differences in meaning. That *Autobiography* is a SH for material on the art and technique of writing an autobiography or for autobiography as a literary genre; whereas, *Autobiographies* is used for a collection of autobiographies not limited to a place or class.

Biography as a common subdivision can be used to divide any life account or biography of an individual; or material on the lives of groups of persons as a class by locality, ethnicity, nationality, profession, gender or any other prominent class characteristic. As a professional group it is applicable to professionals such as scientists, mathematicians, painters, librarians, World War II veterans, kings and rulers, freedom fighters, or to a gender, women. It is equally applicable to groups of persons by race, nationality, or ethnicity such as Africans, Americans, Indians, South America, Indians of South America in Brazil, Bengalis, South Indians, Baverians, and to miscellaneous groups, *e.g.* Handicapped children.

Individual Biographies

A SH for the biography of any individual is in the form of a personal name heading divided by the common subdivision *Biography*. Person's name is to be transcribed in the form prescribed by the AACR - 2. *For example*, A book on the life of Mrs. Indira Gandhi will get the SH.

Gandhi, Indira, 1919–1984 – Biography

Key headings of individual persons such as *Shakespeare, William 1564-1612* or people such as *Indians of North America* may serve as models.

Headings for individual biographies are direct, and are not placed in the class to which the biographies may belong. *For example* for a book on the life of Elizabeth Taylor the SH will be:

Taylor, Elizabeth, 1930 – Biography

Here there is no need of any heading like

American actors – Biography

Or

Actress – Biography

For memorials, reminiscences, individual autobiographies common subdivision Biography or *Personal narratives* may be used. For letters of individuals the common subdivision "Correspondence" may be used. *For example,* Collected letters of S. R. Ranganathan.

Ranganathan, S. R. 1892-1972 – Correspondence

Diary of Anne Frank

Frank, Anne, 1929-1945–Diary

Story of Florence Nightingale

Nightingale, Florence, 1820-1910–Biography

My Presidential Years by V. Venkataraman

Venkataraman, V., 1905 – Biography.

Here the subdivision Biography will be used as there is no common subdivision autobiography.
Similarly

A librarian looks back; Autobiography of S. R. Ranganathan" will get the SH:

Ranganathan, S.R., 1892-1972–Biography

"A backward glance over the trodden roads" by Walt Whitman will get the SH

Whitman, Walt, 1819-1892–Biography

It is quite obvious that such biographies, autobiographies, memoirs will also deal with the subject/event with which the biography remained associated. In such cases an additional subject heading will be in order and quite useful to access the related material. For the book *My Presidential years* another appropriate heading will be.

Presidents – India – Biography

It has been coined on the analogy of the key heading:

Presidents–U.S. Another related and apt, heading for this book is:

India–History, 1985-1990.

Collective Biographies

For a collection of biographies or biographical directories or dictionaries there are many situations. Here collection means an aggregate of *more than three biographies*. If it is a collection of two biographies, then the book will have two separate SHs, one each for each biography. If it is a collection of general biographies not limited to any place, profession or defineable class of people then the general heading *Biography* from the List is used:

Biography 920

Use for collection of biographies not limited to one country or to one group or class of persons. Materials on the art of writing a biography are entered under

Biography as a literary form.

Of course the heading Biography may further be specified by any commonly used subdivision. Let us say our title is :

International Who's who
or Marquis Who's who

For both the works the appropriate SH is Biography – Dictionary

(*Dictionary is a common subdivision.*)

One hundred great lives will get the SH:

Biography

As the arrangement in the above document is not in dictionary form.

Collective biographies of persons belonging to a place, region

For collection of biographies belonging to a region, locality, country, the place itself is the heading. For this key heading could be *United States – Biography* and so on .On this pattern we may coin headings like :

India – Biography – Dictionary

Tokyo – Biography – Dictionary

Dictionary is a commonly used subdivision
Let us take another title

Who's who in Asia. Its SH is
Asia – Biography

Similarly

United States – Biography – Portrait

This heading has been coined as per instructions given against the SA instruction of the SH Biography:

Biography 920

________ __________

________ __________

SA subjects and names of places with the subdivision *Biography*; ethnic groups, classes of persons, and individual literary authors with the subdivision *Biography* or *Correspondence*; and names of diseases, events, and wars with the subdivision *Personal narratives*, to be added as needed.

Moreover, *Asia* is also a listed subject heading. Therefore, specifying it by the common subdivision "Biography" we get:

Asia – Biography

It may be noted that here the common subdivision Dictionary cannot be added as Biography and Dictionary both come from the list of commonly used subdivisions: of these only one is to be used.

Take another example

A Biographical Dictionary of women in Spain

Women–Spain–Biography

Since the subject pertains to a country, so we looked under the United States–women. There we are directed to *women–United States*; so our heading will be:

Women – Spain

This heading may further be subdivided by common subdivision Biography.

Hence the SH is:

Women – Spain – Biography

Here again the common subdivision *Dictionary* cannot be added:

Groups of persons by Racial, national ethnic groups: The subdivision Biography may be added to a class of persons by race, nationality or ethnicity:

Biographical Directory of Arabs
Arabs – Biography
Biographical dictionary of Jews

Jews–Biography

Similarly

Blacks–Biography
Biographies of African Americans in Ohio
African Americans–Ohio–Biography
Biographies of Sikhs in United States
Sikhs are a religious group.

Here there is no entry under Sikhs. Though entries for Muslims, Hindus, Jews and Christian are there. Under *Muslims* we have instructions to divide it geographically. Using this analogy liberally we coin the SH

Sikhs – United States

To this add the common subdivision *Biography*

Sikhs – United States – Biography

Similarly, we may have:

Hindus – England – Biography

Groups of persons by Profession

Collective biographies of a group of persons by profession are entered under their profession. *For example*, scientists, Historians, Engineers, Philosophers, Physicians, Sailors, Surgeons, Teachers, Painters, Sports persons, Publishers, or any other professionals form their own class for collective biography. Names of these professions may be divided by the subdivision "Biography".

For example:

International who's who of poets
Poetry – Biography
Biographies of children who are writers/authors
Child authors – Biography
Who's who of Scientists
Science – Biography
Ten Great Economists
Economics – Biography

Let us have a title "Biographical Dictionary of the French men and women of Science". Since it pertains to a country, so we look under United States, as United States - Science.

There we are directed to use

Science – United States

So our corresponding heading will be

Science – France

This heading can be further subdivided by the common subdivision *Biography*. Hence our appropriate SH is:

Science – France – Biography

Who's who of Indian Army Officers

By looking under the United States we hit at the SH

United States. Army

By adding subdivision *Biography* and replacing the US by India we get the heading

India. Army – Biography

Similarly, let us take another title

Great Parliamentarians of India

For this the SH is

India. Parliament – Biography

Biographies of Rajya Sabha Members will get the SH

India. Parliament. Rajya Sabha – Biography

Biographical Dictionary of Indian Scientists:

Science – India – Biography

Biographical Dictionary of German Musicians

Search under United States draws a blank. Then we look under Musician. Thereunder the SA direction we are permitted that musicians of particular countries are to be added when needed on the pattern of *American musicians*. Therefore our heading will be:

German Musicians

To this we add the common subdivision Biography to get

German musicians – Biography

Of course the other common subdivision "Dictionary" cannot be added

Similarly;

Lives of French statesmen

Will get the SH:

Statesmen – France – Biography

In case there is no term to denote the professionals or practitioners of a subject then the term for the subject itself may be used and may be further subdivided:

For example:

Who's who of Science teachers will get the SH

Science – Study and teaching – Biography

Take another example

Who's who of Indian librarians

First we look under the term *Librarians.* The term exists but there is no instruction to divide it geographically. Since it pertains to a country so we look under *United States*, there we hit the non-preferred headings *United States – Libraries.* There we are directed to look under *Libraries – United States.* Going there we also find the SH *Libraries* which may be divided geographically.

Hence, our interim SH will be: *Libraries – India*

To this we add the common subdivision Biography to get the SH

Libraries – India – Biography

Similarly International who's who of Cricket will get the SH

Cricket – Biography

Take another title:

Who's who of Indian politicians

Here there are two ways to proceed.

1 Look under the United States as the subject pertains to a country, *viz.*, India.
2 Directly try under the heading "Politicians"

Both the approaches take us through and yield the same result. By taking the second approach we arrive at the heading.

Politicians (May subdiv.Geog.)

By subdividing it by India we get

Politicians – India

To this we add the common subdivision Biography to get the succinct SH:

Politicians – India – Biography

Similarly we may have SHs:

Politicians – Asia – Biography
Politicians – Karnataka – Biography
Politicians – Bangalore – Biography

Individual's Autobiographies

In case of an individual's autobiography the SH consisting of the name of the autobiography with the subdivision Biography seems quite superfluous, as the main entry is already under the author's name in the same form. In a dictionary catalogues all the author, subject, title, and other entries are filed in one sequence. Therefore both the author and subject entries will file together at the same place. Hence, the subject entry will be superfluous. In case of a divided catalogue, the subject entry may be required as usual.

Some related SHs

Autobiographies
Autobiography
Autobiographical fiction

Biographical films
Biographical fiction
Biographical radio programmes
Biographical television programmes
Biography as a literary form
Genealogy
Portraits
Religious biography

Commonly used subdivisions related to biography are:

Anecdotes
Case studies
Chronology
Correspondence
Diaries
Obituaries
Personal narratives

Summary

Biographies, autobiographies, biographical dictionaries or directories of persons by locality, profession, race, ethnicity, nationality and religion present interesting cases for coining their subject headings. Individual's biographies or autobiographies are entered under biographee's name in AACR-2 form subdivided by the common subdivision *Biography.* In a dictionary catalogue an individual's autobiography may not be given any SH as it will only duplicate the main entry. Collective biographies of persons regardless of place and profession are entered under the heading Biography.

Following the key headings for a country, state and city, collection of biographies confined to a region are entered under the place name with the subdivision Biography *e.g. Finland–Biography, Helsinki–Biography.* Collective biographies of person by profession are entered under the name of the subject, *for example*, Musicians–Biography; Biochemists – Biography. Collective biographies of persons by race or nationality, ethnicity are entered under the name of the class/group with a subdivision Biography; *e.g.* Jews – Biography, Sikhs–Biography. The SH *Biography* is used for collection of biographies, while *Biography as a literary form* is used for the art and technique of biography writing. Similarly *SH Autobiographies* is used for collection of more than three autobiographies not confined by any place, profession or class, while *Autobiography* is used for the art and technique of autobiography writing, or as a literary genre.

Thus, a lot of common sense, and ability to judge individual cases, in light of the Sears' provisions, are required for assigning subject headings to collective and individual biographical writings.

Exercise

Formulate subject headings for the following titles:

1. Who's who in the world
2. Who's who in Asia
3. Lives of some great kings and queens of the world.
4. Biographical dictionary of freedom fighters of India
5. Dictionary of Oriental biography
6. A Biographical dictionary of scientists.
7. Biographies of Indian prime ministers
8. The Insider; An autobiographical novel by P V Narsimhan Rao-1921- a former Prime Minister of India.
9. Life of Rajiv Gandhi (1942-1991) in pictures by Sonia Gandhi.
10. French composers : a biographical dictionary.